# How to Live with Yourself and Automatically and Simply Love Yourself to Pure Freedom, Health, Wealth, and Relationship Success

# How to Live with Yourself and Automatically and Simply Love Yourself to Pure Freedom, Health, Wealth, and Relationship Success

**The fastest way known to man to a Final Solution to all problems. A truly and absolutely practical how-to guide**

David Cameron Gikandi

**To order additional copies of this book, contact:**
Xlibris Corporation
1-888-795-4274
www.Xlibris.com
Orders@Xlibris.com
41121

# Contents

To Life, From Life.

This is a way,

But it is not the only way.

You may use it,

But follow your own way.

You are your own best way.

This book is about Being Yourself.

# Part 1

## The Practice

# Self-Improvement Begins with Self-Acceptance

"I want to get better," you say. "I want to get better in my health, in my relationships, in my finances, in my spirituality, in social situations, with my body."

You desire self-improvement in various areas of your life.

In fact, you may even have struggled with yourself for years, trying to change some things unsuccessfully. You may have tried everything! And nothing really worked.

Have you ever said to yourself, "I have all the knowledge, tools, courses, and help necessary! Why can't I seem to achieve the life I want even when I have everything I need to make the changes? Why does it look so easy for some people and so difficult for others including myself? After all, we all have access to the same knowledge, the same resources, and all that."

Why, why, why?

I will tell you why. No, I will do one better. I will show you why.

Have you ever heard people talk about being blocked? Being blocked internally? Having a blockage that is preventing them from achieving their dreams?

What is a blockage exactly?

It is a pattern of handling energy; specifically it is a holding pattern better known as resistance.

Have a look at this diagram which represents you in an area in which you may be facing a blockage:

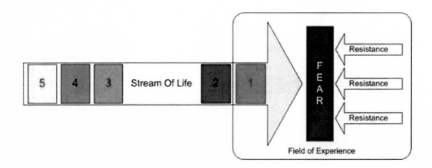

Before we discuss the diagram, let us define the parts that it is made up of.

As you can see, on the right hand side, there is a pink box labeled Field of Experience. This represents what you are experiencing at that moment in time, the Here, Now. You are generally not aware of whatever exists outside your field of experience (which can also be called your field of awareness).

There is also a red box labeled 1 which represents a particular feeling/experience that you tend to avoid. For example, some people are afraid of rejection; and they have conditioned themselves, over the years, to believe that whenever they approach a certain type of person or situation, they will be rejected. And they have come to believe that rejection is BAD, and it makes them a bad person who is undesirable. And so they try their best to avoid feeling rejection. For some people, this issue is very powerful in their psyche. They really see rejection as a painful and bad thing, while for other people, rejection is a blip that is barely noticeable; and it doesn't disturb them at all. Anyway, the red box labeled 1 represents whatever feeling/experience you fear.

You will also notice some arrows on the right side that are labeled Resistance. They are pushing against box 1 and a column of fear. Fear = False Evidence Appearing Real = an attempt to avoid pain = an incorrect conclusion that a certain feeling will produce pain/ rejection = an attempt to reject that part of you that feels that certain feeling before it causes you the pain you fear.

Box 1, along with boxes 2, 3, 4, and 5, is in a large arrow flowing toward and into your field of experience/awareness. This arrow represents the Stream of Life. Stream of Life = Experience = Feeling. Why is experience the same as life and feeling? Well, think about it. The only thing that keeps something real is the feeling! Without the feeling, there would be no experience, and thus no reality. Your entire experience (and hence knowledge or awareness) of reality is composed of feelings. **Experience is feeling**. Very simple.

Now here is where it gets interesting. Imagine now that box 5 represents your desired experience, such as wealth, a good relationship whereby you can effortlessly give and accept love from your partner, etc. Box 5 is that thing you have always wanted but never seemed to be able to get. Let us see how, if you maintain the resistance, your life will look like next year . . .

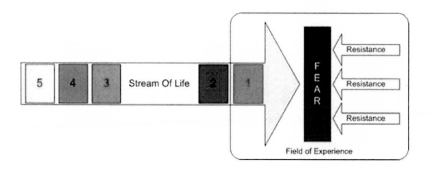

And next year . . .

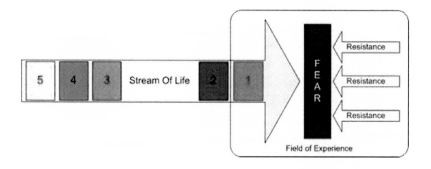

And next year . . .

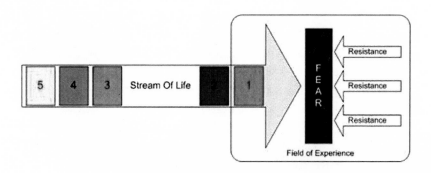

You see? Your very own resistance maintains the status quo. Nothing changes. You are blocking the stream of life from progressing through your field of experience. You will never reach box 5 unless you go through boxes 1 through 4 first.

Now let us take a pause here and see how you actually resist. **How is it you resist?** Well, the two most common ways that you resist are the following:

1. You attack and attempt to stop, change, or kill (eliminate) the event that triggers the feelings you are trying to avoid feeling (e.g., you scream at the other person to change their behavior or you hide or dodge the person or the place, and so on).

2. You suppress your feelings using distractions such as tensing your body, TV, work, drugs, sex, food, driving, sports, or whatever. These things are not bad. No one is saying they are bad. The point is, you can employ just about any activity to suppress feelings, and that then becomes bad for your growth.

So you end up doing one of the above or both so as to avoid feeling that which you are afraid of feeling. This is how resistance works.

Now see what happens when the resistance is eliminated:

This year . . .

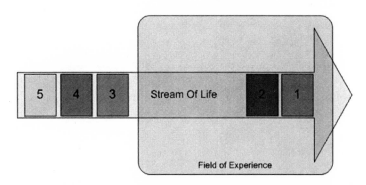

As you can see, the stream is progressing well through the field of experience. Box 1 has been felt/experienced and is on its way out. Box 2 just entered into the field of experience, and box 3 is on the way in. there is growth. There is progress. It was accepted. It was allowed. It was given space to be. And it was, and because everything changes, it moved on. The stream of life is like a river; it flows by bringing ever-new experiences if it isn't blocked.

Now let us see what happens in the next moment . . .

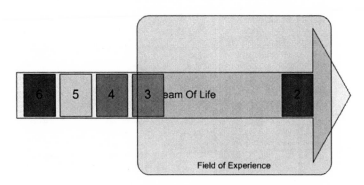

And next moment . . .

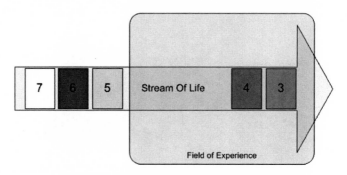

And the next moment . . .

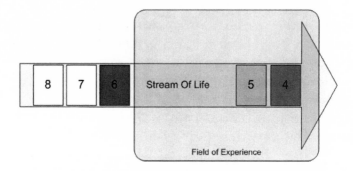

Wow! All that change has happened in moments, not years! So what happens next year? This . . .

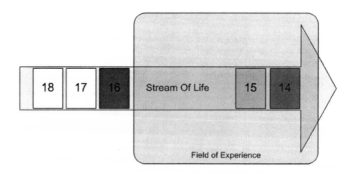

Things sure do move fast when there isn't any resistance, when there aren't any blockages!

So now we know a blockage is simply the habit of avoiding to feel a certain feeling. It is that simple! Yes, yes, I agree, the root causes for such a habit could be as complex as a difficult childhood or a traumatic event. Regardless of the "cause," all blockages are the same, and that is they are the unwillingness or avoidance to feel a certain feeling for fear that it will cause pain and make the person "bad."

Resistance is the opposite of acceptance. When you have acceptance,

1. You DO NOT attack or attempt to stop, change, or kill (eliminate) the event that triggers the feelings you are trying to avoid feeling.

2. You DO NOT suppress your feelings using distractions such as tensing your body, TV, work, drugs, sex, food, driving, sports, or whatever.

**Here is a statement that will guide you in identifying your resistance:** Negative feelings (and by negative we *only* mean whatever doesn't feel good to you) always indicate resistance. Pain and suffering always indicate resistance. In all cases, it comes from your judgment that something is BAD, it shouldn't exist. And this judgment in turn comes from a previous, often covert, self-judgment that you are BAD (hence unacceptable, unworthy of love) if you partake in this experience. The negative self-identity comes first. In other words, you first believed that you are BAD (hence unacceptable, unworthy of love) if you felt a certain way or did a certain thing; and almost immediately, you projected the BAD to that feeling or activity. Do you see how that works? It appears that the thing or feeling is independently bad. But in actual fact, it is you who decided it BAD the moment you decided you were BAD if you felt or did that thing. And all somethings, all things, are experiences. And all experiences are feelings. Without feeling, there is no experience. Hence, negativity is always an attempt to resist or kill a feeling. BAD = shouldn't = eliminate. Your husband is not the problem, lack of money or that new car or house is not the problem, your health is not the problem, your appearance is not the problem, George Bush is not the problem, Osama bin Laden is not the problem, your employer is not the problem. The only problem is that you don't wish to feel a certain feeling, and you will try to do whatever it takes not to feel it. Yet the only way out of your predicament is to first feel that which you don't wish to feel, move through it; and then an automatic transformation of all will occur, and a new way is born.

OK, so what exactly does the statement "self-improvement begins with self-acceptance" mean? And how does it relate to the above diagrams? Let us move on and we will see.

# Acceptance = Unconditional Love = Space = Allowing

These are all the same things. Acceptance is the same thing as a love. Love is the same thing as space. Space is the same thing as allowing. Whenever you practice the art of allowing, you are practicing acceptance. You are practicing love. You are giving space for things to be.

Often people ask, "What is love?"

When someone asks you to love something, they are asking you to give it space to be.

They are asking you to allow it to be.

They are asking you to accept it (not necessarily agree with it, but accept it as part of life, part of the greater whole).

Therefore, whenever you find yourself wondering how to love something, simply remember that all you have to do is to accept it, to give its space, to let it be. This does not mean that you have to agree with it. Nevertheless, love is equal to acceptance.

Acceptance = Unconditional Love = Space = Allowing

It is as simple as that.

> *Always fall in with what you are asked to accept. Fall in with it and turn it your way.*

> **—Robert Frost**

Acceptance = Unconditional Love = Space = Allowing

*We are raised on comparison; our education is based on it; so is our culture. So we struggle to be someone other than who we are.*

**—J. Krishnamurti**

*Learning to love yourself is the greatest love of all.*

**—Whitney Houston**

So what is its opposite? The opposite of allowing is resistance.

Accepting yourself is the simple key that transforms this . . .

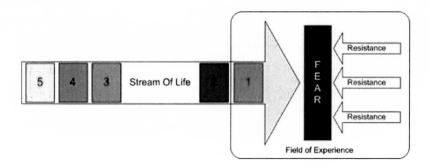

into this . . .

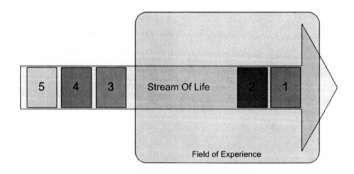

Once again, **accepting yourself is what will release you**. It is so simple. You have heard it said a million times that love is the greatest power of all. They are not talking about romantic love. They are talking about acceptance (accepting what Is), space (giving space to what Is), allowing (allowing what Is to be). It is the opposite of resistance.

So what exactly is accepting yourself? How exactly, do you practice it? How do you change from a habit of resistance to one of natural acceptance and flow? Of letting go? How? How? How?

You will see just how in a moment.

# CLARITY IS THE END
# POINT, THE REWARD

So what is the point of doing this practice?

Well, beyond the fact that you feel better immediately, the supreme benefit is that you end up at clarity.

The end point is clarity; at clarity you can have what is known as a Strong Thought. A strong thought is one which has no opposition. You have moved beyond doubt, conflict, and so on. It is no longer an "if," or a hope. It is no longer theory or concepts. You have moved beyond faith. You now know.

You know.

You just know it.

And so It Is.

You become an unobstructed creator of your reality, at peace and with power. Remember that all obstacles that you face actually originate from within your being, even though they may seem to come from outside of you. At clarity, you are generating no more obstacles.

When you can clearly focus on your desire without any inner obstructions, you create life miraculously, unopposed! Acceptance is the gateway to focus; when you stop fighting, you have peace and clarity. Focus is achieved by releasing (via acceptance), and this frees you to feel good and focus on what you want and move on.

# How to Live with Yourself and Automatically and Simply Love Yourself to Pure Freedom, Health, Wealth, and Relationship Success

*Three are the dwellings of the sons and daughters of Man. Thought, feeling and body. When the three become one, you will say to this mountain "move" and the mountain will move.*

**—The Kabbalah**

# What Else to Expect during and after the Process

As you do the releasing, the letting go, the allowing, certain things will happen to your body and your world. Some will happen fairly rapidly while others may take a while and happen without you even noticing.

Why do they happen? Because you are living in a new way! When you move from resistance to allowing, you are moving to a new way of living. Therefore, it is only natural for things to change around you as well. Remember, having and being are the same thing in different guises, two sides of the same coin. You cannot separate having and being. What you are, so is your world.

The most noticeable of these changes concern the following:

1. **Body**. You may experience visible changes in your body. For some people, they lose weight or add muscle or find that their shoulders no longer slouch, or their frame changes. Some people experience a day or two of a skin rash in a particular area of their body as old; buried irritations surface and move away, and then it goes. Others find that they cry and let go for a whole afternoon one day, and then they feel massively free from an old weight. Others find that an old tension or chronic pain vanishes. For others even, they may get a running stomach for a while as old beliefs move out, and then the running stomach will stop all on its own, and a new you without the old beliefs will emerge. With every change in beliefs, you find that your body goes through some minor or major change. In fact, and I must warn you now, sometimes you may find that the body seems to go into a dis-ease for a short period during the transition and then reemerges even healthier

than before! Whatever happens, don't worry about it. Let it pass; it's a good thing. The body has its wisdom, a wisdom that exceeds the wisdom of your doctor. Remember, your doctor had to go to medical school to know how the heart works, but your heart just knows how it works all by itself; in fact, it even knows far more than the doctor. So yes, there is a time and place for your doctor. He or she is useful and of great service. But never, ever, forget that your body is wiser, and it also knows what to do.

2. **Perspective, mindset, and emotions**. Your emotions, mindset, and perspective will change. Again, each person will experience the change differently. But the key thing here is that you will start thinking differently, feeling differently. Certain thoughts will disappear, and they will be replaced with new ones. You will start feeling differently. You may, for example, go through a period whereby you feel relaxed and then perhaps even ungrounded and pointless as the transition happens; and then it will come a time where you will enter a new predominant feeling point whereby you feel free, unbounded, and happy. You will also see things differently. For example, things that scared you will no longer scare you. Things that made you stressed or uncomfortable will not even register. Things that you missed seeing, such as opportunities, will now become easily and readily apparent. Certain things that were difficult to learn will now become easy. Old habits that were entrenched may suddenly fall away all on their own (some habits and indulgencies are actually tools that are used in the resistance pattern, and when that resistance pattern drops, the habit drops also automatically). You will gain a certain new freedom and more.

3. **Outer world**. Your material world will also change. Again, this will be personal, so I cannot tell you how yours will change specifically. But for example, some people find that old negative relationships with others magically transform into the positive. The guy you have been having a deep argument with for years suddenly calls you, and the two of you somehow bury the hatchet and make peace in minutes. For others, it may be that the financial problem you have been struggling with for a while magically disappears, and a new level of financial stability is established seemingly magically. Or a new business opportunity or career may emerge out of the

blue. Perhaps you might find a very loved and dear new pet (dog, cat, etc.) coming into your life that will make you very happy. Or you may get a new relationship partner. There are no direct and predictable lines to some of these things; only that new forms ("things") come into your life that correspond with the new perspective and feeling point.

When will these changes happen? And will they happen all at once? I can't tell you that. No one can tell you that. It is part of life, the mystery of the path. So don't try to find an answer to exactly what path your changes will take. Relax. It's all good. They will unfold in the best way possible for you and the greater whole. It is all very divine and well.

# HOW TO AUTOMATICALLY AND SIMPLY LOVE/ACCEPT/ ALLOW/SPACE YOURSELF (HOW TO LET GO)

It is all very simple. Very simple indeed. So why doesn't everyone already do it naturally?

Because, over time, in certain areas of their lives, people have become attached to the satisfaction/dissatisfaction of certain experiences. We will look at attachment (craving) later on. For now, just know that the practice itself is very simple, very natural; and it is what you are naturally born to do. As you will soon see, it is in fact the most natural and effortless thing you can do once you get the hang of it.

So without further delay, here is how you can automatically and simply love yourself into pure freedom, health, wealth, relationship, and spiritual success:

First, it is important to realize that you are only inhibited in the areas where you have a block. In areas where you don't have a block (resistance), things are easy for you. For example, some people find it easy to make friends but not money (they have fears of scarcity, life trust issues, or whatever), while others find it easy to make money but not friends (they have fear of rejection, unworthy feelings that they are unacceptable, or whatever).

So when we say "love yourself," what we mean is "love the part of yourself that you have pushed away."

How do you tell which part it is that you have pushed away? The part that is blocked?

Easy! You look for where you have negative feelings, and by negative I mean feelings that don't feel good to you. Feelings that don't feel good to you. Any feeling. For example, if you love sex (it feels good) but you feel guilty for doing it (feels bad), the bad feeling indicates a blockage. If you love money (it feels good) but you are afraid of losing it or not having any (it feels bad), the bad feeling indicates a blockage, a resistance. It isn't money or sex that is bad. No. It is a piece of your feelings about it that isn't supportive of life and growth. That bad feeling keeps you in the cycle of "failure."

That bad feeling is what you call negativity. It isn't bad per se, but it isn't supportive of growth. Bad is a perspective.

So now you know how to identify a negative issue (a blockage).

The next question then is, how do you instantly solve any negative issue?

Well, you follow these steps:

1. Pretend that what you are worrying about has already happened. Adjust its space-time attributes.

2. Feel all the emotions, observing the emotions passing through from a position of detachment.

3. Accept it and accept yourself.

4. Embrace the unknown.

5. From your new self-perspective, choose anew.

Let us visit each of these steps in detail so that they may be clear.

## Step 1: Pretend That What You Are Worrying About Has Already Happened. Adjust Its Space-Time Attributes.

Have you noticed how worry (fear) is structured? It is always future based. You never worry about the past or the present (right Here, right Now). You always worry (fear) about what is yet to come.

In terms of time, fear is future based. In other words, if you look at any of your fears, they are always about something that isn't happening right Here, right Now at this exact moment. Fear cannot possibly exist about something that is in your present. It is always a "What will happen to me if" construct. Even if someone were to put a gun to your head right now, you would fear the possibility that in the very near future, they will pull the trigger. That is why a threat is no longer effective once it is carried out. Fear is always about something that hasn't happened yet (it may be just about to happen, but it hasn't happened yet). You also don't fear things that have already happened, things that are in the past. So that is the time-based nature of fear, or worry.

In terms of space, fear is finite. It occupies a limited space with boundaries. If you focus on that area only, fear can encompass your entire attention to the point that all you are thinking about is your fears, and you completely forget that life has many more things that are far greater that the limited item you fear. If you step back a little, you will see the bigger picture, and your fear will lessen simply because your attention will not be 100 percent on your fear. Imagine that you have one hundred attention units to dedicate. If you dedicate all one hundred to that which you fear, you will be encompassed by your fears. If you step back and look at the bigger picture, you will automatically be dedicating less attention units to that which you fear. Zoom out and see the bigger picture that includes the rest of life.

Now let us complete the technique. How do you best release yourself from that which you fear, big or small?

What is the fastest, most effective way to overcome fear?

It is as simple as this: adjust your space-time perspective. That's it. If you mess with the space-time characteristics of your fear, you will automatically denature it.

Here is the exact way of doing that, step-by-step:

Draw, in your imagination, whatever you fear into the Here, Now. For example, let us assume that you are worried about losing your job or your spouse. That is a future event. Now pretend that it has happened already. That instantly eliminates your having to dodge it, to avoid it. It enables you to stop fighting to avoid it happening. So close your eyes and completely pretend it has happened already. That which you fear is no longer in the future, but it has now happened already. That is all there is to it. Pretend it has already happened; it happened a few minutes ago.

**What is the purpose of this step?** This step enables you to face your fear right here, right now. It disengages your mind and emotions from trying to come up with strategies to dodge the fear. And hence, it frees you from the grueling and distracting activity called worry. This is the first step to freedom. Once you don't have to spend attention and energy on worry, you are clear to move on.

## Step 2: Feel All the Emotions, Observing the Emotions Passing Through from a Position of Detachment.

Feel the feelings you would feel assuming it has happened. Is it shame, anger, vulnerability, grief, guilt, embarrassment? What feelings would you feel if it happens? As you draw the future into the present and fully pretend it has happened, allow yourself to feel absolutely everything that you imagine you would feel if that which you fear actually happened. Whatever it is you are avoiding feeling if that which you fear were to happen, feel it now.

There is a technique you can use to make sure that you do feel fully. This technique involves you disengaging your attention from your thoughts and putting it into your feelings. People use thinking as a way of avoiding feeling. So to minimize this, put your head down and feel the feeling in your stomach or chest or wherever else the feeling is. Literally lower your head; drop it so you are looking down. Close your eyes if that helps, although it isn't necessary. Drop your head and let your attention move away from your head region and into your stomach, chest, and the rest of the body; and feel the emotions running through your nervous system and around you. Put your attention on the feelings.

Let yourself feel fully. Accept whatever you feel and let it flow (flow = release, the opposite of blocking). Instead of trying to fix what you feel, just let go and watch. You are not here to fix the emotion but to observe it. There is nothing to fix here at this stage. Let the feelings be, let them flow, and observe them. Also let your body react as it wishes to. If you twitch, let it twitch. If you shake, let it shake. If you cry, let it cry (yes, even if you are a "big man" who shouldn't cry, let your body cry if it so wishes). Let it be. You may feel as if you are losing control; that is the point. Let your beingness be what it is. Control is what got you into problems in the first place, so don't try to control anything. Simply watch and observe what emotions are there, let them flow, and let the body react to them as it may.

Observe the emotions passing through from a position of detachment. Acting is the nature of body, thinking is nature of mind, observing (watching) is the nature of the Soul. This is where the release finally starts to happen. Consider emotion as phenomenon passing through instead of as something that you label good or bad, positive or negative. Why? Because if it is good, you are going to want to hold on to it; and if it is bad, you are going to want to suppress it (kill it), and that will stop the releasing process. So simply consider the emotions passing through as phenomenon passing through, and not as good or bad things. This is called detachment.

Your perspective will begin to change. You will start to see things in a different light when you watch from a position of detachment. Don't take the change of perspective lightly. You have to understand the value of perspective. Perspective is very important; in fact it determines how you experience life. It determines the options you see or don't see, and much more. It even determines your biology. What? Are you serious? Yes, your perspective determines your biology. Remember that your biology is controlled by your brain because it is your brain that controls your hormones (growth hormones, insulin regulation, cellular functioning, etc.). And your brain is an interpretation device. Your brain (along with your skin) interprets life, and the result of that interpretation is what you call your perspective, and the effect of it is your life experience. If your interpretation is inaccurate, your biology is adjusted incorrectly. If you're your interpretation is accurate, your biology is adjusted correctly. In fact, your whole life is adjusted based on your interpretation of life. Thus, you must ensure that your interpretation is accurate (seeing things as they truly are).

Accurate? You mean you can interpret life inaccurately? You can have an incorrect perspective? Of course! And if your perspective is incorrect, then everything that you think, feel, or do based on that perspective is incorrect. Remember that not so long ago, people thought the world was flat. They looked out into the horizon, and it appeared to them that the earth ended somewhere far out there; and at the end of the earth, one could possibly fall off the edge and die. Therefore, people did not dare to reach the horizon for fear of falling off the end of the earth. So they stayed where they were. Their perception that the world was flat, that it had an edge (the horizon), kept them from exploring far away from where they were born. It was a limitation that appeared real to them. However, this limitation was not real at all—it was an error in perception. The horizon is not an edge, it is not an end. In fact, you can never reach the horizon because it keeps moving farther away from you the closer you get to it. The horizon is an apparent end, yet it is grounded in infinity (you can never reach it). All of your limitations are horizons. All of them bar none. No exception. Horizons are a mindset. Poverty is a mindset. Wealth is a mindset. Happiness is a mindset. Depression is a mindset. Health is a mindset. Dis-ease is a mindset. It is all a mindset, with its accompanying emotions. The secret is that the mind is limitless, so you truly have no limits except those that you have accepted as real. It is all just a horizon, and no matter how much you chase the horizon, you will never fall off the end of the earth. So chase it!

In summary, feel it and watch it as it is.

**What is the purpose of this step?** This step lets progress through. It allows stored tensions and stored old emotions that weren't allowed to move through and complete their course to do just that. The new cannot come until the old has passed through and you have become empty. Allowing yourself to feel is the only way to let your emotions flow. Once again, allowing yourself to feel is the only way to let emotions flow, and hence avoid blockages. You don't have to engage in the emotion and express it. In other words, if there is anger and a feeling that you want to beat up that guy next door, you don't have to express your anger and beat the guy up. In fact that may not be a good idea. However, you don't deny the presence of anger; instead you let it flow through from the point of an observer. This is the key: be an observer. Watch. Just watch in the same way as you would site by the riverside and watch the stream flow by you, carrying whatever it may carry. Watch. Don't block, don't express, just watch. Initially, it may be new and difficult, but with practice, you will get better and better until it becomes effortless and normal for you.

## Step 3: Accept It and Accept Yourself

**This is the key step**. Now that it has already happened and you are feeling your emotions, accept things as they are, and accept yourself as you are. Stop dodging, pretending, or trying to change life. Just accept. Look inward and say, *Jane* [or whatever your name is], *you are a worthy, good, acceptable person as you are even as these things have happened, and I am proud to be you and happy to know you and spend my life with you. I accept you as you are, and I accept life as it is, and I accept these feelings as they are.* Pause. Feel more. Feel first. Accept. Feel more. Accept more. Don't think! Just feel. And accept.

Remind yourself that this part of you was created by your psyche to protect you from your old fears, that it was trying to do you a favor; and at the time it worked well even though now it is outdated and hindering you. So accept more, saying to yourself, to that part you are feeling, *I'd like to come closer and get to know you better. I hadn't realized this before, but you have been here for me all these years, serving me, trying to protect me, giving me time on earth, and I never really thanked you enough. You have loved me since I was a tiny child, you have struggled often just to ensure my survival, and you have always done your best possible in every circumstance even when you didn't know what to do. I wish to thank you now, deeply, from the bottom of my heart. I love you, and I am proud and happy to be associated with you, to know you, to be with you. Thank you. I love you. You make me proud. Thank you. I love you.* Keep doing this until you are totally intimate with that part, that feeling. Until you feel warm and proud to have such a part in your life. It will happen naturally as long as you maintain openness; you don't really have to do anything except open up and accept it. The rest happens on its own. **You will just feel better out of the blue!** ☺

**What is the purpose of this step?** This step is EXTREMELY important! I repeat: this is a KEY STEP! Why is it so important? Because it reverses your negative identity, your negative perspective of yourself. Here is where you finally realize that you are NOT bad just because you feel this way or are this way. You are NOT bad because you feel embarrassed, or you cannot get that job done, or you cannot provide XYZ for your family, or you are not able to give the affection she wants, or whatever. You are not bad! This identity shift changes everything.

It is the negative self-identity that was holding you down. And now it's gone! Your negative self-identity is antilove; it is self-hatred. Once you say, "I am OK even though . . . It is OK to be unable to . . . ," when you OK yourself as you are, where you are, you have solved your main problem. And remember, you don't have to do anything to OK yourself! Don't try to change anything to be OK. Don't change just yet (we will get to that later, but right now you simply accept yourself as you are). The point is to say to yourself it is OK as is, as you are, where you are, without any change. The whole "I am bad, and it is bad to be bad" crappy idea about yourself goes out the window without any changes being necessary; and you become free, where you are, as you are. This is a key step! Don't worry, if you still wish to change or to get that promotion or get your spouse back or whatever, you can still do that in later steps once you gain clarity. But first you must OK yourself where you are, as you are, no change necessary.

## Step 4: Embrace the Unknown

One of the key features of fear is that you are afraid of what will happen if that which you fear comes to be. Solve this problem by simply embracing the unknown. Admit that life is larger than what you know, and that what you don't know isn't a dangerous thing necessarily even though your fears may tell you it is. The unknown is your friend. Tell yourself that even if you don't know what lies in the unknown, and you will never know until you pass through it, you will be able to go through it OK even if you don't know how. Life will just happen. Feel the fear, but do it anyway. You accept that you are moving to a new place you have never been before, and just as when you travel to a new country or town, you will face unknowns. There is no way out of that; the new is always unknown—that is why it is called new. So you might as well say to yourself that yes, there is much you don't know, and it scares you; but you will never know unless you go, so you might as well feel the fear (if any) and do it anyway. That is embracing the unknown. Remember also that the unknown doesn't necessarily hurt. It is simply the unknown. Your fears aren't telling you the truth; they are simply fears. Chances are that the reality itself will be pleasant. Fear is false evidence appearing real. It is a phantom that you make up in your private thoughts.

**What is the purpose of this step?** This step eases your hesitation to move forward. It puts the new, the unknown, in a friendlier perspective. Often the fear of the unknown, the new, keeps us from being willing to move forward. For example, if your system has become accustomed to suppressing a certain emotion in order to feel safe, and now you are seeking to live a life whereby that emotion is not suppressed, your system will need you to embrace a new way of living for it to move forward. It felt safe with suppression; now tell it that you will still be safe without needing to suppress that emotion. You don't have any experience living in this new way, but that is OK. You will enjoy it eventually, and it is more pleasurable than your fears tell you it is. In other words, it is safe to let go. That is the message.

## Step 5: From Your New Self-Perspective, Choose Anew.

This is the step where you finally get to choose the new, the change you seek. This is the step where you finally become the change that you seek. But don't rush to this step. It is in your best interests to complete the other steps first.

Once you have gained clarity from the previous steps, once you have stopped fighting yourself and fighting with life, you are in a very good position to clearly and easily manifest the new. Whatever it is that you desire, you can achieve; you are the only hindrance there is. And by following the previous steps, you eliminate hindrance (the blocks and resistance).

Creation is something that you are born naturally with. But if it is a formula that you seek, here it is:

Let's keep this simple. As simple as can be. What do you want?

More money? A new house? A nice luxury car? A holiday in France? A new boyfriend or girlfriend? An athletic body? Whatever it is, it is a physical result, is it not? Physicality.

Why? For what feeling? So you can feel secure? Happy? Fulfilled? Whatever the reason is, it so that you can feel good, feel free, and experience satisfaction of some kind. It is to enjoy yourself one way or the other. Feeling.

So how do you get whatever it is that you want in your life, easily? Here is the formula for all creation of one's reality. And trust me; it is as easy as you make it to be. If you complicate it, it gets complicated to that degree. If you keep it as simple as it is, it becomes a seeming miracle, simple yet profoundly powerful, a sign of mastery.

And now, the formula:

## Step 1: Ask

How do you ask, and who do you ask it to? You don't have to address your asking to anything or anyone or any deity. The asking is simply your desire and how you feel about it. It is automatic and natural. All you have to do is to be clear on what you want as clear as you can be. Don't bother about how you will achieve your desire—the way will show up step-by-step automatically. Just be clear only on the end result, not necessarily on the way to get there. What is the end result you desire, exactly? Imagine it has already happened.

Also, forget about what you don't want. Here is why: whatever you are putting your attention on is what is being asked for. Where your attention is indicates what it is you are asking. How it is that you are feeling indicates what it is that you are asking. Your attention and feeling will show you, predictably, what it is you are creating in the future and how it will feel like when you get it.

## Step 2: The Universe Answers

At conception, we are all 90 percent water. You probably know how to have sex. But do you know how to put together a baby from water and all the other elements of nature? No! No scientist in this world today can go grab some water and so on and put together babies. Yet we make them without knowing how!

Here is the magic of the universe. The universe is always expanding, always and in all ways. Eternity and infinity. It expands as a function of answering all the desires of all parts of it (even your individual cells ask through their natural preferences for health, nutrition, bliss, and so on).

Did you know that there are many Nobel laureate quantum physicists that have proven without doubt that the act of observing is what creates that which is being observed? In other words, without doubt, you see what you believe. You create your reality. What you intend to observe is what the universe creates in your experience.

This has been proven by quantum physicists many times over the last few decades. If you would like to explore this in more detail, have a look at the e-book *A Happy Pocket Full of Money* from http://www.imagesofone.com.

Literally, scientifically, the universe creates your desire. It handles the "how." So the more you let go and allow life to unfold as it does, the faster you let creation happen for you. Let go of the how so that you can allow it to come to you in the fastest way possible, including ways you would never have thought about. If you insist on the how, you block other pathways and possibilities. Also, let go of the need, anxiety, insecurity, shame, guilt, or whatever because these feelings only create. Let go internally and externally.

## Step 3: Receive

This is the final step and the one that most people seem to mess up. You must receive. Reception is very much like the way a radio receives its channels. It tunes into the channel. The radio must match itself to the broadcast frequency for you to receive any music from it.

In the same way, you must match yourself to that which you asked for so that you may see it appear in your life and experience it. This is the key. And there are two parts to it:

First and most importantly, match your feelings. How would it feel to have that which you asked for? Feel that now. How would it feel to drive that amazing car or have that amazing partner or that amazing business? Feel that now. Feel good. When you feel fear, anxiety, despair, and so on, you are not in alignment.

Second, act on inspiration and "coincidences." You will notice opportunities cropping up in your days. Take them. If you meet someone who somehow mentions something to do with what you are seeking, follow that clue. If you feel the urge to make a phone call or visit a place, do that. It may take one step or a thousand, and you won't always know how far down the road you have come;

but you are guaranteed to get there if you keep taking one step at a time.

The materials of Abraham by Jerry and Ester Hicks also expand on this simple formula, for those of you who wish to investigate it further. The e-book *A Happy Pocket Full of Money* from http://www.imagesofone.com goes into the actual way that the universe goes about creating your reality and more.

Life is a miracle. When you are not experiencing miracles, you are probably struggling up the hard way to get things done. Share this knowledge with others and talk about it; grow it within your friends. As you do, test it. Test it over and over in all areas of your life, perhaps with the small things first. And as you do, you will notice more evidence of it; and as you practice, you will become better at using it and creating a life of miracles as the norm.

# Part 2

## The Foundations on Which the Practice Is Based

# DEPENDANT ARISING
## (*PRATITYA-SAMUTPADA*)

I would like to share with you something that might help you understand everything that we have talked about in a clear way. The following text has been extracted from *Wikipedia,* the free encyclopedia (http://www.wikipedia.org). It is regarding the doctrine of dependent arising, also called *Pratītyasamutpāda* (Sanskrit) or *Paticcasamuppāda* (Pāli; Tibetan: rten.cing.'brel.bar.'byung.ba).

Now although this text comes from a Buddhist perspective, what it talks about can be applied by anyone regardless of religion. Think of it as psychology rather than religion. You will notice that what they talk about is not a doctrine that can only be followed by Buddhists, but it is more of a description of how phenomenon arises.

The very first time that you read this text, it may not make sense. You will need to read it twice or thrice for these things to make complete sense. It only makes sense as a whole. Hence, the need to read it a few times.

Dependant arising is an important part of Buddhist metaphysics. Common to all schools of Buddhism, it states that phenomena arise together in a mutually interdependent web of cause and effect. It is variously rendered into English as "dependent origination," "conditioned genesis," "dependent coarising," "interdependent arising," etc.

## Dependent Origination

The enlightenment (bodhi) of the Buddha Gautama was simultaneously his liberation from suffering and his insight into the nature of the

45

universe—particularly the nature of the lives of "sentient beings" (principally humans and animals). What the Buddha awakened to (bodhi means "to awaken") was the truth of dependent origination. This is the understanding that any phenomenon "exists" only because of the "existence" of other phenomena in an incredibly complex web of cause and effect covering time past, time present, and time future.

Because all things are thus conditioned and transient (anicca), they have no real independent identity (anatta) so do not truly "exist," though to ordinary, deluded minds this appears to be the case. All phenomena are thus fundamentally insubstantial and "empty" (sunya). Wise human beings who "see things as they are" (*yatha-bhuta-ñana-dassana*) renounce attachment and clinging, transform the energy of desire into awareness and understanding, and eventually transcend the conditioned realm of form, becoming Buddhas or Arahants.

## General Formulation

A general formulation of this concept goes this way:

> With this as condition,
> That arises.
> With this NOT as condition,
> That does NOT arise.

An example to illustrate:

You go on summer holiday to a hot climate, such as Arizona, Spain, or Australia. It's a hot, clear day, and you're sunbathing by the hotel pool with the sun beating down on you. You will begin to feel hot, sweaty, uncomfortable, and soon thirsty. You go get yourself a drink to quench your thirst and think, *It's too hot to sit by the pool today, I'm going back to my hotel room where it's cooler, to read for a while.*

> With "hot summer sun" as condition,
> Sweat, thirst, and discomfort arise.
> With "cool hotel room" as condition,
> Sweat, thirst, and discomfort do NOT arise.

This draws attention to the constant flux of "coming to be and ceasing to be" that is happening all the time. All phenomena are subject to this unending interaction. And since all phenomena are dependent on other phenomena, they are all transient and impermanent.

## Applications

The general formulation has two very well-known applications.

## Four Noble Truths

The first application is to suffering and is known as the Four Noble Truths:

1. *Dukkha*: There is suffering. Suffering is an intrinsic part of life also experienced as dissatisfaction, discontent, unhappiness, impermanence.

2. *Samudaya*: There is a cause of suffering, which is attachment (tanha).

3. *Nirodha*: There is a way out of suffering, which is to eliminate attachment.

4. *Marga*: The path that leads out of suffering is called the Noble Eightfold Path.

## Twelve Nidanas

The other application is to the rebirth process and is known as the Twelve Nidanas or the Twelve Links of Conditioned Existence. In this application of *pratitya-samutpada*, each link is conditioned by the preceding one and itself conditions the succeeding one. These cover three lives:

1. Former Life

   - ignorance
   - activities which produce karma

## 2. Current Life

- consciousness
- name and form (personality or identity)
- the twelve domains (five physical senses + the mind + forms, sounds, . . . , thoughts)
- contact (between objects and the senses)
- sensation (registering the contact)
- desire (for continued contact)
- attachment

## 3. Future Life

- becoming (conception of a new life)
- birth
- old age and death

With respect to the destinies of human beings and animals, dependent origination has a more specific meaning as it describes the process by which such sentient beings incarnate into any given realm and pursue their various worldly projects and activities with all the concomitant suffering involved.

Among these sufferings are ageing and death. Ageing and death are experienced by us because birth and youth have been experienced. Without birth there is no death. One conditions the other in a mutually dependent relationship.

Our becoming in the world, the process of what we call life is conditioned by the attachment and clinging to certain ideas and projects such as having a family or making money. This attachment and clinging in turn cannot exist without craving as its condition.

The Buddha understood that craving comes into being because there is sensation in the body which we experience as pleasant, unpleasant, or neutral.

When we crave certain things such as alcohol, sex, or sweet foods, it is the sensation induced by contact with the desired object that we crave rather than the object itself.

Sensation is caused by contact with such objects of the senses. The contact or impression made upon the senses (manifesting as sensation) is itself dependent upon the six sense organs which themselves are dependent upon a psychophysical entity (the idea of a Self), such that a human being is.

The whole process is summarized by the Buddha as follows:

| English Terms | Sanskrit Terms |
|---|---|
| With Ignorance as condition, Mental Formations arise. | With *Avidyā* as condition, *Saṃskāra* arises. |
| With Mental Formations as condition, Consciousness arises. | With *Saṃskāra* as condition, *Vijñāna* arises. |
| With Consciousness as condition, Name and Form arise. | With *Vijñāna* as condition, *Nāmarūpa* arises. |
| With Name and Form as condition, Sense Gates arise. | With *Nāmarūpa* as condition, *Ṣaḍāyatana* arises. |
| With Sense Gates as condition, Contact arises. | With *Ṣaḍāyatana* as condition, *Sparśa* arises. |
| With Contact as condition, Feeling arises. | With *Sparśa* as condition, *Vedanā* arises. |
| With Feeling as condition, Craving arises. | With *Vedanā* as condition, *Tṛṣṇā* arises. |
| With Craving as condition, Clinging arises. | With *Tṛṣṇā* as condition, *Upādāna* arises. |

| | |
|---|---|
| With Clinging as condition, Becoming arises. | With *Upādāna* as condition, *Bhava* arises. |
| With Becoming as a condition, Birth arises. | With *Bhava* as condition, *Jāti* arises. |
| With Birth as condition, Aging and Dying arise. | With *Jāti* as condition, *Jarāmaraṇa* arises. |

The thrust of the formula is such that when certain conditions are present, they give rise to subsequent conditions, which in turn give rise to other conditions; and the cyclical nature of life in samsara can be seen. This is graphically illustrated in the Bhavacakra (Wheel of Life).

There appears to be widespread misunderstanding of the formula in relation to timescales. Many references made to *Pratītyasamutpāda* are expressed over lifetimes. While this is true in the wider sense, **more practically, this is to be seen as a daily cycle occurring from moment to moment throughout each day**.

Throughout the day we cycle through the conditioned states. The conditioned states give rise to pleasant and unpleasant, desirable and undesirable experiences. We crave the existence of such states if they are pleasant, or we crave their absence if they are unpleasant.

> *Your joy is your sorrow unmasked . . . When you are joyous, look deep into your heart and you shall find that it is only that which has given you sorrow that is giving you joy. When you are sorrowful, look again in your heart, and you shall see that in truth you are weeping for that which has been your delight.*

> **—Kahlil Gibran**

Nibbana (Sanskrit: nirvana) is often conceived of as stopping this cycle. By removing the causes for craving, craving ceases. So with the ceasing of birth, death ceases. With the ceasing of becoming, birth ceases; and so on until with the ceasing of ignorance, no karma is produced, and the whole process of death and rebirth ceases.

In fact the opportunity for change comes between the stages of sensation and desire since as we saw above, it is craving that drives the whole process.

**If one can simply experience sensations without attachment, simply letting the experience be what it is and the emotion be what it is, then craving will not arise; and one can begin to be free from the cycle of birth and death in that area of their life.** (Remember, birth and death here is not referring to physical birth and death but to circumstances in your life.) The problem issues that you face over and over in your life are cyclic, and they are there because of your attachment to the emotions involved in them. Have you noticed how one person seems to have a specific problem area in their life that another person doesn't seem to have? You may have certain problems you have been struggling with all your life that other people don't seem to have, and vice versa. This is the cycle of life and death that we are referring to.

When there is contact with the world (forms, tastes, flavors, thoughts, smells, etc.), that contact develops into feeling. Whether you are conscious of it or not, at this point you have a choice of either letting the contact and feeling be what it is and letting go, or labeling it as satisfactory or dissatisfactory. If you choose to label it as satisfactory or dissatisfactory, then you have one more choice available to you. You can let (dis)satisfaction be (dis)satisfaction and let it go, or you can choose to develop craving (whereby you want to either hold on to the satisfaction or get rid of the dissatisfaction). If you let go, then the cycle doesn't continue. However, if you choose craving, then the cycle from this point on is automatic. Craving will automatically develop into clinging, clinging automatically develops into becoming, becoming automatically develops into birth (an "I" is born to be the clinger in this situation, and from there a "mine" arises). And because all things change and pass on, that which you are clinging to will change; hence suffering and death follow. Everything changes. We live in a duality. Night becomes day. Cold becomes hot. Inability turns into ability and back. Clinging doesn't help because that which you cling to will change anyway.

*Your joy is your sorrow unmasked . . . When you are joyous, look
deep into your heart and you shall find that it is only that which*

*has given you sorrow that is giving you joy. When you are sorrowful, look again in your heart, and you shall see that in truth you are weeping for that which has been your delight.*

**—Kahlil Gibran**

The birth, suffering, and death that we are talking about here are that of a particular identity (ego). Your ego/identity is not a singular, static thing. It is a fluid feeling of self that is composed of many, many identities. You have an identity in relation to any particular thing that you have clinging for. An identity in relation to debt, for example, another in relation to your sense of belonging, another in relation to romantic love—many, many. They arise, live, and die many times, over and over, in your life, each day, in any area where you have clinging. *In areas where you have no clinging, you don't have an identity;* you simply take things as they come and flow without "problems" and without recreating "problems" over and over. **If one can simply experience sensations without attachment, simply letting the experience be what it is and the emotion be what it is, then craving will not arise; and one can begin to be free from the cycle of birth and death in that area of their life.**

*Know thyself.*

—Inscribed at the Oracle of Delphi,
ancient Greece, and regarded
by Socrates as the beginning of wisdom

*Do you really know yourself, or do you only know what you have been conditioned to believe about yourself?*

# YOUR EMOTIONS AND FEELINGS BIND YOU OR LIBERATE YOU. YOUR CHOICE.

You have emotions and feelings. These are two very different things. Emotions are your energy field's reaction to your thoughts. Feelings are communication from your soul/spirit. Instinct, gut feeling, intuition, and so on are all feelings. Feelings are not emotions, although the two are often confused.

Often, even in this very book, we use the word *feelings* while we actually mean to say *emotions*. As a culture, we have become accustomed to using the words *feeling* and *emotion* interchangeably. And so, here, we will not try to change that culture. But it is useful for you to be aware that there are differences between emotions and feelings, even though we may, out of habit, continue to call emotions feelings and vice versa.

Feelings do not arise from your mind, nor are they reactions of your thoughts. Emotions are reactions to your thoughts. Once again, emotions are your energy field's reaction to your thoughts, but feelings are direct communication from your soul/spirit. All communication from the soul, even when it is warning of a potential danger, always carries a feeling of loving and knowing; and it does not have a fear behind it at all. The soul's guidance is always gentle and loving, never fearful.

\*    \*    \*

All feelings and emotions are energy in motion (e-motion). They are in **motion**. As such, every feeling and emotion, if left to freely run its course, will always lead to a greater understanding, a new insight, and so on. Because they are in motion, they must lead to something else; none can be a dead end. When you experience being stuck in an emotion, it is only because you are attempting to resist or block feeling something. All emotions when allowed to run without interference will always lead to love and to the belief that spawned them, making it known to you.

\*     \*     \*

When you allow your emotions to run their cause, you automatically allow your body, mind, and emotions to be in harmony. When you deny your emotions or try to resist or run from them, then you split up your psyche and remove yourself from reality. When you deny them, you automatically also hide from yourself the thoughts and beliefs behind the emotions and even build up body armor (like fat) to hide these emotions and keep them unconscious.

\*     \*     \*

If you find yourself blocking or resisting any emotion, ask yourself what beliefs you hold that are causing the motivation to resist. Ask yourself why you are so afraid of the emotions. See what beliefs you hold that are causing the resistance in the first place.

\*     \*     \*

You must understand that you are **not** your emotions. Make a clear distinction between you and your emotions. You are not your emotions. For example, the feeling "I feel I am a failure" is not a fact of reality but an emotion, and it is not a statement about you but a statement of how you feel. You are not a failure, but if you believe you are, then you will experience that. You are Spirit. You must learn to make a clear distinction between you and your emotions so that you can learn how to work with them deliberately and comfortably. Nevertheless, emotions are valid, and you need to allow them that validity and right to exist even as you recognize that they are not facts about reality.

\*　　\*　　\*

The key to healthy experience of emotions without blocking them is very simple: truth. Simply live from the **truth of your being,** and that is all. At every moment, let the truth of your being express itself. If, for example, you are suddenly very angry with a friend, don't pretend everything is OK and cover your anger with a smile. Instead, state it clearly and truthfully that you are angry and why. You cannot deny the truth of your being and expect positive results (even if you think manipulation will serve you better than truth). Anger, when used clearly and truthfully, is designed to correct imbalances. When you cover it up and dress it with a smile, you deny yourself that healing abilities of it, and you store it within where it festers into an unhealthy and distorted form of itself (such as violence). Whenever you cover up your feelings, you cover up your power and your energy, and you deny yourself the chance to know the *true* reasons behind your anger. The reasons behind the anger only show themselves at the end of expressed anger—you face the anger, and you will face the reasons. Although it may not be apparent, the reason why you think you are angry is often very different from the reason why you really are angry (it is always a fear within that feels threatened and spawns anger in seeming self-defense).

\*　　\*　　\*

Here is another way of looking at feelings and emotions:

> The two halves of the duality of Creation exhibit a constant motion in relation to each other around a central matrix of intent. This might better be described by first imagining God's concept in the form of an immaterial amoeba, a small pre-conscious globe we will label "thought". Just like an amoeba, this minute ball elongates and separates into two equal balls now called individually "thought" and "feeling". Immediately thought and feeling begin to rotate around each other in a tight circle and in so doing these two nuclei wrap around themselves a shell of Clear Light, the primal substance, thus forming the three (the smallest building block) or Germ of Creation. These three having

55

coalesced into a single core imbued with God's Will, that nucleus reaches a critical compression point, its "equation of state" at which point it projects outward a hologram in the shape of the Creator's original intention. The "three in One", or trinity, continue to emit this condensate of primal essence shaped like the intended object, as long as God's thought maintains that particular creation. This final result of the Source's original intent is the fourth cause, what you call matter, but is in reality, solidified consciousness. Allow us to recapitulate: God's singular intent is the first cause; this first cause has two aspects: thought (the masculine) and feeling (the feminine); together they represent the second cause. Notice that we say feeling and not emotion: we will presently explain the difference between the two. The second cause, by circular agitation of the formless void, starts a vibration that incites the Clear Light to respond and envelop the disturbance while simultaneously taking notice of God's design. That is the third cause or trinity which exists for only that single instant before it explodes like a nova into a multi-directional holographic image of the original Will and renders that Will tangible in the concentrated form of consciousness you call matter. That end result is the fourth cause. As for the promised definition of feeling versus emotion: **feeling is the awareness of a connection, whereas emotion is what you experience when you believe that you are separate from the thing with which you interact.**[1]

*   *   *

Fear is always the absence of love, and Truth only resides in love. Therefore, the presence of fear automatically indicates the absence of love and truth. Thus, the fear is always about an imagined outcome; it is an illusion, and it is not founded on truth. Fear is **false evidence appearing real.** Fear is always because of a lack of understanding,

---

[1]    Thespian Michaels and Esmi Fernau, *The Mysteries of Clear Light, First Trilogy, A Timeless Legacy*

and so it points to what is not yet understood about life. Fear is the emotion of being separated, being disconnected from the greater Reality. Yet separation does not exist except as an illusion of perception, and therefore, fear is an illusion because Oneness is all there is in Reality. As separation does not exist, then its emotion (fear) is also an illusion, just as it is.

\*     \*     \*

Fear is dispelled in the light of understanding, of love. You do not "get rid" of fear, destroy it, run from it. None of these will take it away. Only understanding of the fear, which leads to knowing the love that is missing, will transform fear, expose it for the cloud of illusion it really is and dispel it as if it were a simple veil of smoke. When you run away from fear, you are simply denying your own power and responsibility and ensuring that you remain stuck.

\*     \*     \*

On the other side of fear is your own denied power.

\*     \*     \*

**Fear is always a wall that separates you from another part of yourself**. It is an illusion of separation from which many other illusions are built. A great way to examine your fear and understand it is to face it and talk to it. Face it by feeling it fully. How does that wall of fear feel, taste, smell, and so on? What is it all about? What is it threatening to do? Feel it. Then talk to it; hold a conversation with it. Then switch over to the other side of the fear. So look at what is on the other side of your fear. In other words, look at the threat itself, that which you are fearing. Talk to it as well. Then talk to yourself. Keep this conversation going between you, the wall of fear, and what lies beyond the wall until there is an agreement between the three parts. This internal dialog will reveal much. Then act. Even if you are still feeling the fear, do what you fear to do anyway. This is the last step, and once you act, you will see that the fear was an illusion all along. As with anything, it takes practice, and you get better at this each time you practice it.

\* \* \*

**Using fear as your ally is the best way to go about fear.** As you know, fear is the opposite (absence) of love, and so it is the literal experience of being disconnected from Who You Really Are. Fear, therefore, can teach you a lot about your beliefs and so on. The first step to using fear as your ally is to admit that you are afraid if you are afraid. Just say, *Yes, I am feeling afraid.* This will put you into the truth of the situation while at the same time making it clear to you that you are not your fear, but you have a feeling of fear. You realize that the statement "I am afraid" is not accurate because you are not your fear. Instead, "I am feeling afraid" reflects the truth that you are not your feelings, but you have these feelings for now. You will then be able to notice the next thing, that fear is also the experience of holding back (denying) your other feelings (and other parts of yourself) because you feel they are overwhelming you in one way or the other (perhaps coming on too fast, to strong, etc.). Once you notice that, you will then also notice that most fear is based purely on assumptions about these feelings. Most fear is never about what is happening right here, right now. It is about what **might** be. It is the projection of what happened in the past into the future. In other words, when you are in fear, you are not in the moment and are instead assuming (making it up) that what happened in the past will happen to you again in the future. And this assumption is a thought, and all thoughts have emotions attached to them. It is these emotions that you wish to hold back because last time you felt them, they were too much for you at that level of understanding at the time. You will also notice that you are greatly exaggerating and magnifying the imagined situation; you are building up a terrifying worst-case scenario, gathering and making up "evidence" that supports this fearful assumption and getting rid of everything that doesn't. You will also notice that your assumption is just an assumption that lives privately only in your mind. Realize that the past was a time with completely different variables. Every moment is fresh and doesn't have to repeat the past **unless** you make it so by your thoughts, words, and actions, by what you put your attention to. Once you get to all these realizations, you can then face your admitted fear and walk through it by doing what you fear. This will allow you, finally, to process the feelings and emotions you have been denying and holding back; and from that you will gain new understanding, growth and overcome your fear! Once you have done that, you will notice that you are no longer projecting, in this case, no longer fearing. You will notice that in this matter, you are now able to stay in the present. And you will then discover the secret behind all fears: that when you stay in the present, no fear can find you.

*   *   *

Here is a puzzle for your mind. See if you can settle comfortably into it. Infinity and eternity are the Reality of Life (or Source or God or whatever term you like), and Life is all there is; Life (God) is everywhere. But never mind that. The point is, even science, quantum physics, has proven that time is only an illusionary construct of the mind, a perceptual and conceptual illusion (as the idea that the earth is flat was a commonly held "truth," which we now know it isn't). "The earth, no matter how flat it appears to be, is round." No way! A long time ago, many people were convinced that the earth was flat. When they said "till the ends of the earth," they meant it. They had no way of knowing it was round—no reference in terms of position or travel speed that was good enough to reveal the truth to them. You needed to be high enough or travel fast enough to know that the earth is round. Until then, this insight escaped them. As for time, Albert Einstein said that "time, no matter how persistent, is an illusion." Eternity and infinity, on the other hand, are Realities. So now take one of your current fears. Bring it to mind. Notice that it is a worry, a fear about the future. It is always about something that you imagine happening a moment or more beyond Right Now, and it is something you have deemed undesirable and overpowering. This is fear. Fear requires time. Even if you were held at gunpoint, you would only fear getting shot "later" (even one second from Now). Time. Without time, no fear. Time is an illusion. In other words, everything you can imagine happening, all possibilities (infinity), are happening right Here, Now (eternity). Ah, but you are not aware of them all at once! All possible states of you, you doing and being all possible things, are happening right Now, "somewhere" in the Multiverse. That is eternity, infinity. But you are only aware of "one of you." That is "time." So now, about your fear again. If you understood what we just talked about, then you will understand that this thing that you fear so, so, so much is happening "somewhere else" right Now—and that is the only moment it will ever Really happen. It cannot possibly happen "tomorrow"—only Now. And it is, anyway as are all possibilities and probabilities. Now understand the concept of choice. It is very simple. There are only choices. You will only experience "the you that is going through the feared experience" if you choose to. If you don't choose to, you won't. Your world is maintained by your thoughts. Your imagination is the navigation vehicle you use to move between all the possibilities of the Multiverse. And you don't have to keep thinking the way you do.

*   *   *

> *Fear, faced and felt with its bodily sensations and the thoughts that go along with it, will automatically bring about its own state of resolution. The conscious system of beliefs behind the impediment will be illuminated, and you will realize that you feel a certain way because you believe an idea that causes and justifies such a reaction.*

**—Seth**

*   *   *

Negative thoughts: should I fear and avoid them or embrace them?

Can negative thoughts create negative experiences? Yes. All thoughts create at some level.

Does that mean that you should fear negative thoughts or try hard to avoid them? No.

Why?

First of all, let us clarify and say that obviously it is far more efficient and pleasurable to have positive thoughts instead of negative ones. So from that point of view, you can say that negative thoughts should be avoided. However, that is assuming you are clear and have conscious choice in the matter. However, if you find that you are somehow

60

driven to think negatively in a certain area, don't spend energy and emotions trying your best to suppress these negative thoughts. Instead, embrace them, accept them, remind yourself that these thoughts are beliefs about reality and not facts of life; and then ask yourself why you are having these thoughts. Why? The answer will be an insight into the beliefs that you hold that are causing you to think negatively. This understanding will allow you to change that belief, and this will automatically stop the barrage of negative thoughts in that area. Remember, your thoughts and imagination always follow your beliefs, so that is where you should work on change (at the belief level). But you cannot arrive at this understanding as long as you are still resisting yourself, and that is why you should embrace negative thoughts and use them to lead you to the limiting beliefs you hold. When used that way, negative thoughts become friendly beacons that guide you toward limiting beliefs you have held unconsciously or consciously.

In summary, think positively; but if you find yourself thinking negatively, accept that, but ask yourself what belief is behind the negativity. This is the fastest and surest way to increasingly empower your life and free yourself from negativity.

*   *   *

The energy of natural aggression is behind all creativity, all life. Nevertheless, natural aggression has been largely misunderstood in our current civilization. Natural aggression is not only the driving force behind love but also the basis of all emotion and is one of nature's best and most powerful self-healing energies. Misunderstanding it can cause a person to be afraid of certain emotions and block himself or herself from living or self-healing.

*   *   *

Love is not opposed to natural aggression. Also, natural aggression has nothing to do with physical violence. In all of life, a creative and loving thrust forward is always needed to perpetuate motion or creation (in other words, to activate love). This creative, loving thrust forward is natural aggression.

61

*　　*　　*

When you deny yourself the experience of natural aggression, you fall into all sorts of problems. For example, if you see natural aggression as wrong, then you will not feel free to feel and express anger when appropriate. Anger, when used naturally without distortion, always aims at correcting an imbalance. In fact, natural anger rarely lasts longer than half a minute in most day-to-day cases and never leads to violence. However, if you believe natural aggression is wrong, then you will tend to suppress your anger; and it will build up until it blows up in an exaggerated display of anger that may involve violence. The distortion of natural aggression is what causes unhealthy emotional reactions. Also, if you deny yourself the expression of natural aggression, you will tend to see power as threatening and bad, and love as weak and powerless (and because you tend to think of yourself as good, you will automatically see yourself as powerless because of this distorted view of power you have formed). You will also be afraid of experiencing powerful emotions and in that way greatly cut yourself off from a full and creative life. Even diseases and painful life situations often come into being because an individual has denied themselves their own power to act, and as soon as the power to act is seized again, these problems resolve themselves. **Every creature is built with an innate desire to choose and act on that choice. When, for any reason, that power is suppressed, an imbalance must occur; and self-correction, in one form or another, always attempts to happen.** Natural aggression is a very normal and natural part of all life, and its denial is a root cause of many problems including violence. Violence happens not because of natural aggression but because of the denial and distortion of natural aggression. Whenever you deny yourself your own power, your abilities, you create beliefs and habits that make you live and perceive as if you are powerless and an external entity holds power over you. Even on a global scale, you can see this denial and projection of power when you look at the structure of governments, religions, societies, gangs, regimes, and so on.

Energy has consciousness that is part of it. For example, a thought is energy, and it has its own consciousness that carries its experience. A cell in your body has its own consciousness, a feeling of what it is. You have your own consciousness, a feeling of what you are.

62

Emotions are energy in motion, with its own consciousness, a feeling of what it is.

As energy moves, it interacts with other energy, lives its course; and its consciousness moves through its own healthy cycle of "birth, life, death." This is how consciousness at all levels grows through a cycle of initiation, experience, conclusion, and understanding. Let us now focus on the energy that is your aura.

Every time you experience an event, your energy flows in certain natural ways within your aura. For example, you have the emotions of the experience, you go through the experience, you understand it and integrate it; and then release it and move on, keeping the wisdom you have gained. This whole process happens smoothly and automatically if not obstructed. **However, whenever you repress or interfere with this process, you literally have that part of you (that "cluster" of energy) stuck in time! This is what a blockage is.**

Every time you interfere with the flow of energy, you create or enhance a blockage. People interfere or try to stop the flow of energy due to their fear of being hurt. Whenever they experience an event that they classify as painful and unwanted, and they then try to avoid feeling the emotions associated with that event and expressing themselves fully, they literally freeze that event in both energy and time. Most blockages are formed between conception and the age of seven. After that, they are enhanced and rendered unconscious through further attempts to avoid feeling and expressing oneself during events that one considers painful. People create blocks because at the time, it relieves them of the pain of facing the event fully and truly. However, when they stop the flow of energy so as to avoid pain, they halt this energy as it were at the time and prevent it from going through its full cycle of unhindered and clear initiation, experience, conclusion, and understanding. For example, assume a person at the age of two years faced an experience that they considered painful and that they chose to not experience and express fully. That part of their psyche that was involved with that experience will not mature as the rest of the person does. Instead, it will be frozen in the same state that it was in at the age of two. The person, when faced with similar situations, will react just as they did at the age of two. They will have unreasonable fears, they will perceive the situation as they did when they were two, they will misunderstand it in the same way. In other words, even if they are now forty years old, they will face all similar situations just as they did when they were two. And that is because that part of their psyche was frozen in time and consciousness, never having the freedom to flow normally and grow with the rest of the person. To unblock himself or herself, this person has to heal this at the level it was created. In other words, they have to face their fear, allow themselves to fully feel all the emotions of similar events as they come, and allow themselves to express themselves fully regarding the situation. They have to feel their fear instead of turning away and manipulating the situation and running as usual. They have to stand their ground (it's OK to admit and feel fear, but have the courage to stand your ground) and face and feel their fear, face and feel all the other emotions that would follow once they have faced their fear, and then express themselves fully. What they would then find out once they have faced that fear is that their fear was unjustified, that it was based on a past and outdated moment, that in the new moment everything can be different; and that they can effortlessly handle such situations with power, integrity, and maturity! That part of their psyche will then grow and catch up with the rest of the person, perhaps instantly or perhaps in a short while.

Because almost all people at this stage of our evolution have a wounded inner child, almost all people have dozens of frozen energy-consciousness clusters in various areas. In any particular day, as you cycle through various aspects of life and interact with different people, you are constantly and automatically switching between your adult self and your various frozen energy, consciousness-time blocks. So in one situation you may act like an adult, in another you will act just as you did when you were five years old, in another you will act as you did when you were nine, in another as you did when you were in your mother's womb, and so on. The work of healing the wounded inner child is actually the work of freeing all of the frozen parts of the psyche, liberating them and bringing them together as one accepted Whole.

Another thing to know about frozen energy-consciousness-time clusters is that they attract like energy and as such recreate similar events. Well, all energy attracts like energy. But now you start to see why people seem to have the same kind of experiences (the ones they fear and hate) happening to them repeatedly. It is because of these frozen energy-consciousness clusters. Because they are being held in the aura instead of being given way to naturally unfold and transform, they keep "repeating the past," which is what they are (a frozen past), until they are allowed full expression and released.

At the root of the forming of all blocks is an erroneous image conclusion, an error in thinking, a belief that we are less than we are.

## From Kahlil Gibran's *The Prophet*: on Love

Then said Almitra, Speak to us of Love.

And he raised his head and looked upon the people, and there fell a stillness upon them. And with a great voice he said:

When love beckons to you, follow him,

Though his ways are hard and steep.

And when his wings enfold you yield to him,

Though the sword hidden among his pinions may wound you.

And when he speaks to you believe in him,

Though his voice may shatter your dreams as the north wind lays waste the garden.

For even as love crowns you so shall he crucify you.

Even as he is for your growth so is he for your pruning.

Even as he ascends to your height and caresses your tenderest branches that quiver in the sun,

So shall he descend to your roots and shake them in their clinging to the earth.

Like sheaves of corn he gathers you unto himself.

He threshes you to make you naked.

He sifts you to free you from your husks.

He grinds you to whiteness.

He kneads you until you are pliant;

And then he assigns you to his sacred fire, that you may become sacred bread for God's sacred feast.

All these things shall love do unto you that you may know the secrets of your heart, and in that knowledge become a fragment of Life's heart.

But if in your fear you would seek only love's peace and love's pleasure,

Then it is better for you that you cover your nakedness and pass out of love's threshing-floor,

Into the seasonless world where you shall laugh, but not all of your laughter, and weep, but not all of your tears.

Love gives naught but itself and takes naught but from itself.

Love possesses not nor would it be possessed;

For love is sufficient unto love.

When you love you should not say, "God is in my heart," but rather, "I am in the heart of God."

And think not you can direct the course of love, for love, if it finds you worthy, directs your course.

Love has no other desire but to fulfill itself.

But if you love and must needs have desires, let these be your desires:

To melt and be like a running brook that sings its melody to the night.

To know the pain of too much tenderness.

To be wounded by your own understanding of love;

And to bleed willingly and joyfully.

To wake at dawn with a winged heart and give thanks for another day of loving;

To rest at the noon hour and meditate love's ecstasy;

To return home at eventide with gratitude;

And then to sleep with a prayer for the beloved in your heart and a song of praise upon your lips.

## From Kahlil Gibran's *The Prophet*: on Pain

And a woman spoke, saying, Tell us of Pain.

And he said:

Your pain is the breaking of the shell that encloses your understanding.

Even as the stone of the fruit must break, that its heart may stand in the sun, so must you know pain.

And could you keep your heart in wonder at the daily miracles of your life, your pain would not seem less wondrous than your joy;

And you would accept the seasons of your heart, even as you have always accepted the seasons that pass over your fields.

And you would watch with serenity through the winters of your grief.

Much of your pain is self-chosen.

It is the bitter potion by which the physician within you heals your sick self.

Therefore trust the physician, and drink his remedy in silence and tranquility:

For his hand, though heavy and hard, is guided by the tender hand of the Unseen,

And the cup he brings, though it burn your lips, has been fashioned of the clay which the Potter has moistened with His own sacred tears.

## From Kahlil Gibran's *The Prophet*: on Pleasure

Then a hermit, who visited the city once a year, came forth and said, Speak to us of Pleasure.

And he answered, saying:

Pleasure is a freedom-song,

But it is not freedom.

It is the blossoming of your desires,

But it is not their fruit.

It is a depth calling unto a height,

But it is not the deep nor the high.

It is the caged taking wing,

But it is not space encompassed.

Aye, in very truth, pleasure is a freedom-song.

And I fain would have you sing it with fullness of heart; yet I would not have you lose your hearts in the singing.

Some of your youth seek pleasure as if it were all, and they are judged and rebuked.

I would not judge nor rebuke them. I would have them seek.

For they shall find pleasure, but not her alone;

Seven are her sisters, and the least of them is more beautiful than pleasure.

Have you not heard of the man who was digging in the earth for roots and found a treasure?

And some of your elders remember pleasures with regret like wrongs committed in drunkenness.

But regret is the beclouding of the mind and not its chastisement.

They should remember their pleasures with gratitude, as they would the harvest of a summer.

Yet if it comforts them to regret, let them be comforted.

And there are among you those who are neither young to seek nor old to remember;

And in their fear of seeking and remembering they shun all pleasures, lest they neglect the spirit or offend against it.

But even in their foregoing is their pleasure.

And thus they too find a treasure though they dig for roots with quivering hands.

But tell me, who is he that can offend the spirit?

Shall the nightingale offend the stillness of the night, or the firefly the stars?

And shall your flame or your smoke burden the wind?

Think you the spirit is a still pool which you can trouble with a staff?

Oftentimes in denying yourself pleasure you do but store the desire in the recesses of your being.

Who knows but that which seems omitted today, waits for tomorrow?

Even your body knows its heritage and its rightful need and will not be deceived.

And your body is the harp of your soul,

And it is yours to bring forth sweet music from it or confused sounds.

And now you ask in your heart, "How shall we distinguish that which is good in pleasure from that which is not good?"

Go to your fields and your gardens, and you shall learn that it is the pleasure of the bee to gather honey of the flower,

But it is also the pleasure of the flower to yield its honey to the bee.

For to the bee a flower is a fountain of life,

And to the flower a bee is a messenger of love,

And to both, bee and flower, the giving and the receiving of pleasure is a need and an ecstasy.

People of Orphalese, be in your pleasures like the flowers and the bees.

# Your Judgments, the Origin of Your Pain and Suffering

Many perspectives exist on judgment; the world sees judgment in many different ways, does it not? Well, we will look at a different perspective over here. And it is this:

*No judgment exists outside of your mind.*

That is to say, judgment only exists in your private thoughts, in the private thoughts of John, of Jane, and of any other person who chooses to have judgment. Outside of these private thoughts, no one is judging. Not the universe, not the gods or God, nowhere else. How?

First, what is judgment? It is the attempt to murder What Is. That sounds harsh, but look again. Let us say something has happened or someone has done something. You then look at this thing or person; and you judge, using whatever reasons, that this person or thing is bad or shouldn't have happened. Consider that for a while. Something Is, it is already in the universe, the universe and Life has given it space and life to exist as it Is; but you come along and say it should not be as it Is. In other words, in the real universe, it exists, it Is, it is ever part of All That Is. But in your private thoughts, in the little model of the universe you have created in your private thoughts, what Is should not be or is wrong! The Real universe says it is valid, it exists, it is given life, it Is; but your private model of the universe attempts to wipe it off. And this gives you great discomfort, doesn't it? This is the load of judgment. Consider also that someone else may find that which you judge as wrong to be perfectly OK. And the universe itself allowed it to be and even gave it life. The idea of universal judgment is a projection, and only a projection, of personal judgment. No judgment exists outside your mind. Turn the view around, and this time let us assume that someone has judged you. Have you ever been judged? If you are like almost everybody else, someone has probably judged you before plenty of times. So here you are, existing in full as you are, as Is. Then along comes someone with their own personal issues and their own private mental model of how the universe should be, and they look at you and notice that a part of you doesn't fit into their private mental model of the universe. This gives them insecurity, and in their desire to get rid of that fear, they angrily turn on you and say that a part of you should not exist! Now do you see how ridiculous judgment is when you turn it around? Especially to a child, it just doesn't make sense. As a child, you are trying something for the first time in your life, innocently experimenting, with no past experience to even give you a hint of what the outcome may be. It is all very natural and normal for you to experiment. It is not good or bad; it just Is. Then comes this screaming adult with their private model of the universe, and they scream at you and judge you and/or your drive desire and action as "bad," "it shouldn't have happened, what were you thinking!" Hmmmm.

Now have you noticed that in your life you live in reality and in an illusion? In the moment of Now, right Here, look around. The universe is alive. This is where life is. Now you also have a private mental world you carry around. It is complete with fake voices, fake sights, fake people—the voices in your mind, those things you call thinking. Have you noticed how you actually walk around deep in "thought," dealing with your private world, talking with the imaginary figures in there, and then you actually react as if they were real? People even have arguments with real people based on the imaginary conversations they had in their imaginary world of illusion! That private mental world that is shared by no one but yourself is the world of illusion; yet you project it out and live part of it in the real world.

There is no conflict in the universe except in your private "thoughts," in the illusion. In Reality, there is only One, and that One is at peace. By conflict we mean something happening that should not happen. We are not talking about natural interactions of life. We are talking about conflict here as it compares to perfection. The universe is eternally perfect, an ever-changing process of perfection. Conflict is only in the human private mental worlds. In Reality, all things are in harmony, working together for the good of All (or God, whatever term you like).

God doesn't judge? Why should she/he? Nothing can exist outside of the Creator, outside of Life. If God is All That Is, Life Itself, why would the Creator judge against a part of Itself, a part that could not have happened without It giving it Life? How can the Creator hate a part of Itself? And what then would be the point of unconditional love? The confusion only comes when you separate the Creator from the creations. But when you view the creations as manifestations of the Creator, as the Creator in various forms, as extensions of the Creator (the child, made in the image and likeness), then you see them as One and the Same Thing, then the idea of God judging collapses and shines through as a human concept. Humans, at least most of them, cannot yet accept a concept of have-no opposition. The perspective they use even when looking at their own lives is that their lives consist of some opposition from outside of themselves (the taxman, the unfriendly neighbor, bad business conditions, the nagging spouse, and so on). The idea of external opposition is firmly in humanity's collective consciousness. It is just an idea. A person can look at their lives from the perspective of them having external opposition seemingly going against their own wishes. But the same person can look at their lives and see that there is indeed no external opposition, that it is not possible for external opposition to exist, and that their whole life situations, including the "opposition," are a manifestation of their whole inner beingness, and as such they are completely unopposed by anything other than themselves. And because they incorrectly see themselves as victims of opposition, they project that to the Creator also, imagining that something in Creation can possibly go against the Creator (how, when they are One?); and furthermore, such an act would deserve judgment and punishment. They cannot imagine that the Creator is One Without Opposition. But the Creator Is One Without Opposition, and All Things are part of All That Is (another way of saying God is everywhere), an extension of the Creator (image and likeness) in various forms, and unconditionally accepted As Is, as they are. In fact, they are given life to be As Is.

*There is no order of difficulty . . . Forget not that it has been your decision to make everything that is natural and easy for you impossible. If you believe . . . is difficult for you, it is because you have become the arbiter of what is possible, and remain unwilling to give place to One Who Knows. The whole belief in order of difficulty . . . is centered on this.*

**—A Course in Miracles**

Life just Is.

And it Is so just for the experience. The experience of It All.

What Is is what Is. When your private model of the universe says what Is should not be, that attempt to end Life doesn't work. Instead it creates a painful load. When someone judges you for doing something you like to do, if you accept that judgment, you carry the pain of judgment (self-hatred). If you don't accept the judgment, then that person has to live with you as you are; and because they cannot accept this, they experience the discomfort of the pain of judgment.

Every judgment carries an unnecessary load. It is an attempt to murder what Is. The load of judgment is toxic emotions which affect other areas of your life. Yet judgment exists only in your private "thoughts." It has been said countless times by the great teachers that have walked this earth: do not judge. And if you find yourself judging, don't judge yourself further for judging.

All your pain comes from judgment, and behind judgment is fear, and behind that fear is a denied part of yourself, and embracing that part releases you from your fear and your tendency to judge and create your pain.

The universe doesn't judge—It Just Is. You often find people saying, "Why do bad things happen to good people? Why does God give this bad guy so much money?" The universe does not have some good/bad judgment system. It is a simple interaction of cause and effect. Ask and it shall be given. The ideas of good and bad were told to you by other people, were they not? Where did they get those ideas?

*   *   *

Let us look at death for a little while. It is a great illustrator of this judgment concept. People look at death as bad. They even imagine that God punishes people for "causing the death of another" (which is, from a different perspective, impossible to do). They sometimes blame "the devil" for people dying naturally. Well, let us see how God has it arranged in one tiny part of the universe: fire ants and the phorid fly!

Fire ants are a species of ants, and the phorid fly is a species of flies. Do you know how the phorid fly perpetuates its species? God has designed things this way: The fly quickly injects its egg into a living ant. This ant walks around as the fly's egg hatches into a larva inside the ant. The larva then starts to eat the ant from inside until it finally kills the ant and emerges as a fly! Why would God create it so that an ant has to die every time a fly is born? To punish the ant for some "bad" things? Many, many species of life live in such symbiotic arrangements. Does this sound cruel? When a person is hit by a car and dies, is that cruel? To whom? To the person? That assumes that they did not, at some level, choose their death, that their death was at the "wrong time," and that what is after death is "bad." Or to God? How? How can something outside of Life's (God's) Will have life to do what is against Life? Where would it get the life to do that? When you locate whom something is "bad" for, you notice that it is privately bad only to the persons that see it that way. From the perspective of Spirit, death is simply a change of energy, change of state. Change is always part of the universe and has always been. It is part of the design of the universe. At any moment, millions of plants, people, insects, and so on are dying—and being born. It is normal. Furthermore, death doesn't affect the Self, the eternal spirit, at all. Most of all, and this is what many great avatars and teachers of humanity have come and tried to remind humanity many, many times, death is an illusion, a construct of the mind. In Reality, all Creation is of everlasting life. To understand this logically is not easy. But many have experienced it in fact. The judgment of death, the fear of death, is very much a human concept, which they then project to God and say that God also has the same ideas as they do.

The basic idea of judgment is this: reality Is alive and allowed in the Universe As It Is, yet in the private mental model of the world, it "should not be." Why? Where did that idea come from? What is behind it?

You are alive in the Universe As You Are, a unique expression of Life, like everything else is; yet in the private mental model of someone else's "thoughts," you shouldn't be as you are, in your uniqueness! That is judgment. The Reality allows you to Be As You Are, gives life to you as you are, but the illusion in someone's thoughts says you should not be. Does that sound reasonable? Especially when you remove the personal story around the event or you look at it at the level of the Whole picture, judgment makes no sense at all.

$$* \quad * \quad *$$

Avoid judging things as right or wrong. Things are just things. Their classification lies in the choice of the observer of these things to classify them as good or bad, right or wrong, fun or not. The minute you judge things, you judge yourself. You also block the hidden gift that an event brings to you.

$$* \quad * \quad *$$

The Taoists have a wonderful way of explaining it using the story of the farmer whose horse ran away.

The farmer's horse ran away; and his neighbor, feeling sorry for this farmer, said to the farmer, "I am sorry that such a bad thing happened to you." The farmer replied, "Don't be, for who knows what is good or bad."

Well, the next day, the horse that ran away came back to the farmer, this time bringing with it a herd of wild horses that it had befriended. The neighbor said to the farmer, "I congratulate you for your good fortune!" The farmer replied, "Don't, for who knows what is good or bad."

Well, the next day the farmer's son tried to mount one of the wild horses and fell, breaking his leg. Again, the neighbor said to the farmer, "I am sorry that such a bad thing happened to you." The farmer replied, "Don't be, for who knows what is good or bad."

The next day soldiers came by to forcefully recruit for the army, but the farmer's son was exempted because of his broken leg.

Now this is just a simple story, but it demonstrates the miracles that Creation works in the most unpredictable and seemingly unconnected ways so that all things work out to perfection.

\*     \*     \*

By some people's perspective, right and wrong exist as universal realities. Yet another perspective is that there is no right or wrong; there just Is. If you can see it this way, then you can also see that you have never done anything wrong in your life, ever. There is no wrong choice. There is only choice and the experience of choice. The idea of a right or wrong choice can only make sense if you take a side, create a story around the choice. It is a private idea that depends on where you stand.

\*     \*     \*

The belief in separation is the root cause of all other errors, the root cause of all your problems. From the belief in separation come other beliefs such as need, lack, fear, and so on. Your life always follows your beliefs; your beliefs create your life experiences. If your mind was to recognize that separation is an illusion created for the sake of self-experience, if it were to recognize that separation is not a reality (and hence cease believing in it), all other limiting beliefs that you hold *because* you believe in separation would fall away. Your life experience would automatically change to reflect this new vision of oneness, love, abundance, no limitations.

\*   \*   \*

Once you start observing your life, you will start to clearly see that you are *not* your beliefs. You are something else that holds beliefs and thus experiences them as they manifest physically. You also start to notice that your reality is a lot more fluid than you thought it was, and that whenever you change your beliefs, it changes as well. Now all your problems are manifestations of limiting beliefs. All limiting beliefs arise only when the belief in separation is still held. Therefore, you truly have only one problem: the belief in separation. But because separation does not exist except as an illusion of perception, you now see that your only problem has been solved, and hence you Really, Truly, have no problems. You only have one problem, the belief in separation. But that problem has already been solved because separation does not exist. All that is required is that you recognize this, and you will experience it (you always experience your beliefs; that is a key principle in this game of self-experience that we are all playing). You do have heaven on earth, truly, but you have to first accept it in mind to experience it physically, as with all things.

\*   \*   \*

Hidden behind most of the problems that people face is self-hatred (to one extent or the other). The opposite of self-hatred is full self-acceptance. One way to know if you have an element of self-hatred is to ask yourself if you accept yourself fully as you are. Most people don't even recognize consciously that they have an element of self-hatred. The struggle to improve one's self-esteem or self-worth indicates the presence of self-hatred. In the absence of self-hatred, there is no need that is felt to "improve" one's self-worth or self-esteem. A person who has full self-acceptance has a drive to better themselves; but this comes from a place of knowing that they are fully perfect and worthy at all time, always, all ways. In other words, their desire to be better comes from a place of self-love and not from a place of guilt, fear, neurosis, or competition. To such people full of self-love and acceptance, "becoming better" means growing, increasing in consciousness and experience. It doesn't mean "ironing out the imperfection."

Self-hatred suppresses and distorts so many functions and energy streams of a person that it is the underlying cause of much suffering and dis-ease.

The psychological cause of self-hatred is found within self-betrayal in childhood. This is how self-hatred forms: Imagine a child growing up under several authority figures (parents, teachers, society, etc.). These figures place expectations of some kind on the child. The child may not be able to meet these expectations perhaps because it isn't ready to, or they may not even be right for the child. In fact, the expectations themselves could be very incorrect. However, the little child doesn't have the reasoning ability developed to analyze these expectations. Even if they were far-fetched or impossible to meet, it wouldn't know. All the child would think is that the parent (or other figure) must be right, and for the child to have love and acceptance, it would assume it must meet these expectations. The child also is eager to please and keep happy those around it, including these authority figures. And so it tries to meet these expectations (willingly or under force as it sometimes is). Whenever it "fails" to meet these imposed expectations, the child may dislike itself for not having been able to do what was expected. It may see itself as the problem, its inability as the cause of its pain and apparent loss of love. In addition to that, the child may wish to express itself regarding the issue (perhaps to say that it doesn't want to participate, that it is afraid, that it is hurt, or whatever). However, if the child's self-expression is further suppressed (say by the parent who is now angry with the child because of this "failure"), it will further hate itself and conclude that this kind of self-expression only leads to more pain. The child now concludes that something must be inherently wrong with it, something that causes it pain. It then hates this part, attempts to hide it, and attempts to build a **mask** (piece of ego) that is designed to protect it. This mask is a set of self-judgments, beliefs, and assumed behavior that attempts to prevent any further similar occurrences. For example, a child who concludes that "expressing love is weak and painful" will create a "tough guy" mask self, complete with beliefs, modes of behavior, set reactions, and a self-judging inner critic. Now whenever the child uses this mask, they may indeed avoid pain, at least initially. In fact, they may even be rewarded with praise by the authority figures. So now the child's psyche is further confused because the mask is being rewarded, which further "proves" to the child that the real self is not good at all and must be masked by something else that "works." This, over time, becomes unconscious and leaves only a trace of dissatisfaction with self, a feeling that "something is wrong with me somewhere." Of course, nothing is wrong with anybody. It is the masks that cause the pain, all the while giving the illusion that they are the solution. The child, even later as a grown-up, doesn't stop to question the expectations of those who were imposing them on it. It doesn't stop to consider that these seemingly right authority figures are themselves people with their own fears, their own erroneous assumptions about life. The child just assumes "they must be right, so I am wrong." Of course, this is far from the truth.

*　　*　　*

*There is nothing wrong with you.*

*　　*　　*

The work of dissolving the mask is the work of recovering the parts of yourself you judged wrong and reclaiming your Wholeness, peace, and power. All this is the result of and leads to self-love.

And there is nothing wrong with people, or with the human condition. If you hold the idea that humans, people, are "bad," then you will find it very hard to hold an idea of you that is self-loving and accepting as well. Remember, in the universe, what you value and put your attention on is always what you experience.

*　　*　　*

The key to all transformation and healing is self-trust. Eventually, you **must** begin to trust yourself. There is no other way. And eventually, you will be forced to because the lack of self-trust brings with it increasing discomfort. So you might as well start to trust yourself right now, here. There is no reason to wait until tomorrow unless you make one up. By nature, you are inherently worthy of trust and trusting. As long as you do not trust yourself, you will fear yourself and find it hard to love yourself. You will not believe or expect any help and power from within you, any information and insights, and so on. As long as you do not trust yourself, you will place yourself under the control and direction of others and simultaneously resent them because you feel you are not living your life but theirs. You will not recognize your uniqueness and will always feel the pressure and need to compare yourself with others, and so you will never be satisfied because comparison between unique things is meaningless in reality. You will always feel as if your experiences and knowing are fake or wrong while that of others are right and real. These are all the results of refusing to trust your self, your being, your feelings, your thoughts, your imagination, yourself. And from these springs a whole host of other difficulties (e.g., control issues, guilt). So trust yourself now, no matter what, just by knowing that all that is within your being is true for you. Be yourself by trusting yourself. This is the key to all healing and transformation—living your truth, the truth of your beingness. You can only do so if you trust it because then you give it value and express it instead of giving other people's truth more value and expression than your own truth. Trust yourself. Any reason, logic, or excuse you have been given in the past as to why you shouldn't trust yourself is just an idea. In truth, you are built, like all Life, to be infinitely trustworthy and intelligent; and you live in a safe universe. How will you know if you don't try it yourself? And whenever you stumble, at least you learn from your own intent, direct experience. There is no failure, only successive moments. The Creator does not create some people as trustworthy and some not—all are trustworthy, and anything contrary to that is a result of conditioning. You learn how to trust yourself by trusting yourself. It might be hard at first, but it gets easier with time, just like learning how to ride a bike.

## From Kahlil Gibran's *The Prophet*: on Joy And Sorrow

Then a woman said, Speak to us of Joy and Sorrow.

And he answered:

Your joy is your sorrow unmasked.

And the selfsame well from which your laughter rises was oftentimes filled with your tears.

And how else can it be?

The deeper that sorrow carves into your being, the more joy you can contain.

Is not the cup that holds your wine the very cup that was burned in the potter's oven?

And is not the lute that soothes your spirit the very wood that was hollowed with knives?

When you are joyous, look deep into your heart and you shall find it is only that which has given you sorrow that is giving you joy.

When you are sorrowful, look again in your heart, and you shall see that in truth you are weeping for that which has been your delight.

Some of you say, "Joy is greater than sorrow," and others say, "Nay, sorrow is the greater."

But I say unto you, they are inseparable.

Together they come, and when one sits alone with you at your board, remember that the other is asleep upon your bed.

Verily you are suspended like scales between your sorrow and your joy.

Only when you are empty are you at standstill and balanced.

When the treasure-keeper lifts you to weigh his gold and his silver, needs must your joy or your sorrow rise or fall.

## From Kahlil Gibran's *The Prophet* on Good and Evil

And one of the elders of the city said, Speak to us of Good and Evil.

And he answered:

Of the good in you I can speak, but not of the evil.

For what is evil but good tortured by its own hunger and thirst?

Verily when good is hungry it seeks food even in dark caves, and when it thirsts it drinks even of dead waters.

You are good when you are one with yourself.

Yet when you are not one with yourself you are not evil.

For a divided house is not a den of thieves; it is only a divided house.

And a ship without rudder may wander aimlessly among perilous isles yet sink not to the bottom.

You are good when you strive to give of yourself.

Yet you are not evil when you seek gain for yourself.

For when you strive for gain you are but a root that clings to the earth and sucks at her breast.

Surely the fruit cannot say to the root, "Be like me, ripe and full and ever giving of your abundance."

For to the fruit giving is a need, as receiving is a need to the root.

You are good when you are fully awake in your speech.

Yet you are not evil when you sleep while your tongue staggers without purpose.

And even stumbling speech may strengthen a weak tongue.

You are good when you walk to your goal firmly and with bold steps.

Yet you are not evil when you go thither limping.

Even those who limp go not backward.

But you who are strong and swift, see that you do not limp before the lame, deeming it kindness.

You are good in countless ways, and you are not evil when you are not good,

You are only loitering and sluggard.

Pity that the stags cannot teach swiftness to the turtles.

In your longing for your giant self lies your goodness: and that longing is in all of you.

But in some of you that longing is a torrent rushing with might to the sea, carrying the secrets of the hillsides and the songs of the forest.

And in others it is a flat stream that loses itself in angles and bends and lingers before it reaches the shore.

But let not him who longs much say to him who longs little, "Wherefore are you slow and halting?"

For the truly good ask not the naked, "Where is your garment?" nor the houseless, "What has befallen your house?"

## From Kahlil Gibran's *The Prophet*: on Crime and Punishment

Then one of the judges of the city stood forth and said,
Speak to us of Crime and Punishment.

And he answered, saying:

It is when your spirit goes wandering upon the wind,

That you, alone and unguarded, commit a wrong unto
others and therefore unto yourself.

And for that wrong committed must you knock and wait a
while unheeded at the gate of the blessed.

Like the ocean is your god-self;

It remains for ever undefiled.

And like the ether it lifts but the winged.

Even like the sun is your god-self;

It knows not the ways of the mole nor seeks it the holes of
the serpent.

But your god-self dwells not alone in your being.

Much in you is still man, and much in you is not yet man,

But a shapeless pigmy that walks asleep in the mist searching
for its own awakening.

And of the man in you would I now speak.

For it is he and not your god-self nor the pigmy in the mist
that knows crime and the punishment of crime.

Oftentimes have I heard you speak of one who commits a wrong as though he were not one of you, but a stranger unto you and an intruder upon your world.

But I say that even as the holy and the righteous cannot rise beyond the highest which is in each one of you,

So the wicked and the weak cannot fall lower than the lowest which is in you also.

And as a single leaf turns not yellow but with the silent knowledge of the whole tree,

So the wrong-doer cannot do wrong without the hidden will of you all.

Like a procession you walk together towards your god-self.

You are the way and the wayfarers.

And when one of you falls down he falls for those behind him, a caution against the stumbling stone.

Aye, and he falls for those ahead of him, who, though faster and surer of foot, yet removed not the stumbling stone.

And this also, though the word lie heavy upon your hearts:

The murdered is not unaccountable for his own murder,

And the robbed is not blameless in being robbed.

The righteous is not innocent of the deeds of the wicked,

And the white-handed is not clean in the doings of the felon.

Yea, the guilty is oftentimes the victim of the injured,

And still more often the condemned is the burden bearer
for the guiltless and unblamed.

You cannot separate the just from the unjust and the good
from the wicked;

For they stand together before the face of the sun even as
the black thread and the white are woven together.

And when the black thread breaks, the weaver shall look
into the whole cloth, and he shall examine the loom also.

If any of you would bring to judgment the unfaithful wife,

Let him also weigh the heart of her husband in scales, and
measure his soul with measurements.

And let him who would lash the offender look unto the
spirit of the offended.

And if any of you would punish in the name of righteousness
and lay the axe unto the evil tree, let him see to its roots;

And verily he will find the roots of the good and the bad,
the fruitful and the fruitless, all entwined together in the
silent heart of the earth.

And you judges who would be just.

What judgment pronounce you upon him who though
honest in the flesh yet is a thief in spirit?

What penalty lay you upon him who slays in the flesh yet is
himself slain in the spirit?

And how prosecute you him who in action is a deceiver
and an oppressor,

Yet who also is aggrieved and outraged?

And how shall you punish those whose remorse is already greater than their misdeeds?

Is not remorse the justice which is administered by that very law which you would fain serve?

Yet you cannot lay remorse upon the innocent nor lift it from the heart of the guilty.

Unbidden shall it call in the night, that men may wake and gaze upon themselves.

And you who would understand justice, how shall you unless you look upon all deeds in the fullness of light?

Only then shall you know that the erect and the fallen are but one man standing in twilight between the night of his pigmy-self and the day of his god self,

And that the corner-stone of the temple is not higher than the lowest stone in its foundation.

# You Create Your Reality. There Is No Other Rule

Now that you know that all things are simply combinations of energy giving an illusion of form to our physical senses, we can move on to a very important law that governs how energy reacts. It is so simple, but by this law shall you begin to master your world.

First, to recap,

> *All things are energy. They are not "made up of" energy. They ARE energy. All things. It is only your set of senses that gives the illusion of form depending on how these senses perceive this energy.*

Now how does this energy work? Well, much can be said about it, but for now, let us look at one of the biggest laws of energy. We will look at it stated scientifically and spiritually:

**Scientific**

> Like energies display harmony, resonance, construction, and attraction. Unlike energies repel, have dissonance, and create destruction. For example, sounds that are in tune with each other form harmonious music. Sounds out of sync with each other destroy each other (wave motion). By nature, like energies attract; unlike energies repel. It is called harmony.
>
> All objects have a vibration, a frequency. Even a human body has a frequency. Brain waves have various frequencies. DNA has a frequency range. Your words have a frequency range.

91

Colors are merely expressions of certain frequencies. Each energy particle has its own frequency. This vibration is what sets off the law of attraction mentioned above. This vibration is the one that dictates whether a particular energy body is in or out of tune with another and therefore whether it will disrupt or build on the other, attract or repel it. Keep this in mind. We shall be referring to your vibration many times throughout. Just before we move on, it is appropriate right now to mention that every state of being you get into changes your vibration frequency. That is why you tend to feel lighter when you are happy, heavier when you are sad and gloomy. The more you move toward love and joy, the higher your vibration. The more you move to fear, the lower it is.

## Spiritual

As you sow, so shall you reap.

Karma.

Law of cause and effect.

Do unto others what you would like to be done unto you.

As we proceed, you shall see numerous ways that this law of attraction comes into play in ways that you would never before have considered. For example, how does criticism and judgment of others hinder your progress? Why do all our religions tell us not to judge one another? That very thing that you are so angry about that is making you feel like judging and criticizing someone else about is setting of a certain vibration in you. Do you see that? And that vibration that you put out will bring back the effects to you, the source. Whatever you try to deny another, you automatically attract that denial to yourself. It is not a punishment being handed down to you. All it is, is this:

All vibrations that you offer come back to you as perfectly corresponding manifestations.

The "downside" of this for you is that any critical thought and emotion that you have toward another person will unfailingly limit your own progress.

The upside is that once you remember to always, in your thoughts, words, emotions, and actions, give the best to others, nothing will be denied to you simply because you will no longer be blocking your own progress; and you will be having a new vibration of abundance hanging around you. Now don't forget that you also count. Give yourself the best, and drop all judgment and criticism of yourself. You cannot clearly create what you desire in your mind if your emotions contradict your thoughts.

The other upside is that no one can enforce anything on you. You will soon see very clearly that nothing you see or experience can be caused by a source outside of you. Your free will, and the law of attraction, guarantees this.

Nothing you see or experience can be caused by a source outside of you, for no one can vibrate for you.

You see, at the moment you may not be conscious and aware of all the thoughts and feelings you have on all levels twenty-four hours a day in your conscious, subconscious, and superconscious parts of you. Therefore, this lack of awareness may make things seem to come from a source outside of you. But in reality, they all spring from either your conscious, subconscious, or superconscious. And you can learn to raise your awareness so that more and more of your decisions are conscious.

However, it is absolutely liberating to know that the whole idea of external assertion is false; it does not exist.

So how do you tell what your vibration is? Simply look at what you are feeling. At every moment, one of the most important questions you should always ask yourself is this:

What am I feeling now?

Notice not only the feelings and emotions at the front of your awareness but also the ones that ride just below your awareness, the ones you have gotten used to and don't even notice anymore.

Notice even the ones you have been avoiding to feel, denying them. The emotions and feelings you have denied and rendered unconscious to your awareness (because you imagine you will feel pain if you feel them, and so you fear them) also still create! These are the source of the things that seem to "happen to you" in your life, the ones where you pretend to be a victim and say, "I didn't ask for this." Really?

This determines what follows in your life. Always be aware of your feeling, and know that you can change it at will. Your feelings indicate to you your vibration, and they predict what will come next unless you change it before the manifestation that would normally follow occurs.

Now that you are getting better at this, here is a simple puzzle that you should be able to solve. Let us say that you are unhappy about your current state of finances. Will that create more or less finances for you?

The answer may be obvious to you by now. It will create less. Why? Because your vibration, your feeling, is "unhappy about finances." This will attract whatever gives evidence of that, meaning that you will find even more events and people that you "think" are making you even more unhappy about your finances. All the time, it is you who is in control. This brings us to another secret about conditions:

Conditions do not exist as external, independent entities. Conditions arise out of a state of being. They do not cause a state of being. They are effects, not causes. Unhappy conditions are created from an unhappy state, not vice versa. You are unhappy because you are unhappy, and you are happy because you are happy.

Therefore, if you are unsatisfied with your finances, the first step to changing that is to have a new attitude of gratitude and satisfaction. From this new state, coupled with new thoughts of wealth and positive expectations, your finances will miraculously and quickly turn around.

OK, it is time for the next lesson in vibration. You now know that the universe, by the law of attraction, brings back to you experiences that match your vibration. It is pure science. Here is the next lesson:

The universe does not care or question why you are vibrating, feeling, in a certain way. It simply brings forth experiences that match your vibration. It does not judge. It simply cooperates 100 percent. That is how much it loves you. You never ask for an apple and get a snake. There is no such thing as not getting what you call forth. When you find yourself thinking that you are not getting what you want, look within to see what hidden beliefs you hold contrary to your desires.

What this means is that it does not matter whether you are vibrating, feeling, a certain way because of something you are actually seeing or simply imagining. A vibration is a vibration regardless of why it is there, and it will be acted upon. The universe does not check first to see whether you are vibrating the way you are because of something you want or not or something real or imagined or something good or bad or whatever. It does not check, and it does not decide whether to match your vibration or not. It simply, always, matches whatever vibration you are giving out and effortlessly brings along a matching experience.

Let us recap.

Energy is the carrier of thought and memory. Energy can never be destroyed, and thoughts and memories are carried forever by the particles that store them. Thought is the shaping of an idea, which then gets expressed as an event by the energy that holds it. The event is created so that the consciousness that originated the thought (which is you) may have the experience of the thought. Finally, the memory of this experience is recorded in the energy.

All this recording, carrying, and creating happens through vibration. It is the vibration tone of the involved energy particles that records the thoughts and memories (much like a music record), and it is this very same vibration that, through resonance and attraction, brings together all that is required to create the event.

Energy cannot be destroyed, as you know from your physics class. Thoughts are forever. Eternity is all there is, world without end. Every thought you have ever had, every action you have ever taken, ever word spoken is still out there encoded for eternity on those infinite and indestructible energy "particles." Everything that has ever been created and will ever be created, all of infinity, exists right Now. You simply choose which part you desire to experience. That is the extent of the power of this universe and of your Self.

You make your own reality. There is no other rule.

\*     \*     \*

Each person has a unique thumbprint, unique DNA, unique astrology chart, unique appearance, unique heart frequencies—everything is unique! Each person also experiences a unique reality that is different from anyone else's! Comparing two people is as futile and irrelevant as comparing an apple and an orange. As long as you compare yourself with another, you will never be satisfied. In nature, everything is unique, and the power is found within working from the point of your uniqueness, not by conforming and losing yourself. There is no one right way for everybody, or even for two people. Trust yourself and honor others. Trust the individual and unique divine spark within you; and honor the fact that everyone else is, like you, divinely unique.

\*     \*     \*

Whenever you reject any aspect of your physical human experience, you also reject an aspect of your spirit and mind. Whenever you reject any aspect of your spirit, you also reject an aspect of your physical human experience and mind. Whenever you reject any aspect of your mind, you also reject an aspect of your spirit and physical human experience. Body, mind, and spirit are one, a trinity in unity.

\*     \*     \*

A key principle to keep in mind, and one that will give you the ability to respond in life and create your life as you desire, is that **you create your own reality from the present moment only**. The present moment is your only point of power, and it is here that you create your reality, consciously and unconsciously. Once you realize this, you also realize no external source can push an outcome to you that you did not attract and create at some level. You also realize, then, that you are responsible for your life; and you are not a victim. Taking up this responsibility automatically gives you response ability. And this is where life mastery begins in intensity.

There are some two very simple questions which, once you get their answers, can change your life dramatically for the better. This is so because these two questions relate to absolutely everything that you experience and create in your life.

Everything in this universe runs under universal laws that never err even once. To be in the flow—to live in harmony with these laws—leads you to being all-round prosperous. Such harmony results in effortless well-being and prosperity simply because you would be riding the currents that build and maintain all creation. But now the two questions as follows:

What are universal laws? (Hint: they are like glue.)

Why are there any universal laws? (The answer is more profound than you think it is!)

Let us now look at the answer to both of these questions. Once you have the answer, you will begin to see how dramatically your life can be empowered by your new insight.

To begin to understand it all, one must consider, briefly, why the universe exists in the first place. The reason behind the creation of creation can be summarized as follows: In the absence of that which is not, That Which Is, is not. In other words, the Original Source that some people refer to as God was all that there was; there was nothing else. Now that presented a problem.

This Infinite Being knew itself to be all-powerful and infinite; but without something to compare itself against, so to speak, there was no way of experiencing that infinity and power. It lives in a realm of absolute, where comparison, and therefore experience, is impossible. You need something to experience against for experience to occur. So It possessed Knowing but needed Experience to complete Being.

The solution was therefore to individuate Itself into seemingly separate life-forms so that each of these life-forms could experience itself in relation to the others. Hence the world of relativity and experience was born out of that desire to Know Itself. When people say, "God is everywhere," that statement has more literal meaning than they imagine. Literally, everything is an extension of that Original Force, an expression of an aspect of It All. It creates by extending Itself, ensuring that all creation is in the image and likeness of Itself in essence, and that essence expresses itself in a variety of forms. And this is where the universal laws come in.

Now you see that the primary purpose of creation was for Life to experience Itself, for You to experience Yourself. If you watch the cycle of creation closely, you will notice that it follows this birth-life-death cycle: From the unified nonphysical to the individuated nonphysical to the individuated physical to the individuated nonphysical to the unified nonphysical. Through this process, a Being comes to know Itself by materializing knowingness (thought), then experiencing that thought and its effect, then testing, choosing, and converting that knowing from experience into being. For example, if you have never experienced happiness and I told you that being happy feels great, you would know in your mind what I mean, conceptually; but you wouldn't really complete that knowledge without first experiencing happiness and becoming happy.

The Creator had to ensure that this cycle completes itself automatically and serves each purpose without ever making a mistake. In other words, the laws were built to (1) glue the system together through all those transitions and (2) ensure that the knowing-experiencing-being system of evolution, growth, and learning works perfectly with predictable results so that all Its Children of all forms may get to grow and Know Themselves as extensions of the Original without fail, no matter how long it took, and to do so within a system of free will.

To put it in another way, a universal law is a bond that connects all experience so as to achieve total knowing.

It was a big project, but it worked! Now let us look at some of these laws and see specifically how they apply.

Before we start, it is important to know that these laws do not punish you for breaking them; they cannot be broken. Suffering simply comes up when you try to ride against them. It is amazing how much time and effort can be saved by riding along with them. You literally collapse time when you are in the flow.

**Law of gratitude.** You have heard it many times that an attitude of gratitude has the power to get you realizing your dreams at record speed. Why? Because gratitude completes the cycle of knowing. Remember, you cannot know what is without knowing what is not. What you like and what you hate are two ends of the same thing. For example, if you like being with your spouse and hate being separated from them, realize that you are working within the same essence, which is your spouse. It is because of the moments of absence that you appreciate and recognize the moments of presence. When you are grateful for both what you like and what you don' t like, you complete the knowingness, and you are released from having to experience what you don' t like. This cannot be explained logically, but some very significant shifts occur in your mind and soul (and you can feel this releasing shift) whenever you are genuinely grateful for all things, even the ones you don' t like. Gratitude will speed you through your growth and success more than any amount of hard work ever can. Gratitude completes the lesson, and as a statement of completion rings that tone of success, pulling to you the end result desired. Another way to put it is that you cannot leave a situation permanently unless you appreciate the gifts it brings you, and all situations bring a gift, no matter how terrible the situation may appear to be. This law ensures that you will always complete your knowing and embrace all that is before moving on.

**Law of attraction.** This law states that you attract whatever you put your attention to. The point of this law is to establish the creative power of thought. Whatever you put in your conscious or subconscious mind, you attract into your experience. This law is very much tied to the law of cause and effect. It is the law that establishes you as a being made in the image and likeness of the Creator, with a mind that possesses the same creative properties. Before you learn that you indeed have this power, your mind will wonder and raise many thoughts, some of which conflict and attack you. At this level, things such as doubt and preferences exist, for you do not think you are responsible and powerful enough to be the creator of your reality. As you watch your life and begin to see the link between your thoughts and your experiences, you become a deliberate thinker, and you no longer think negative, doubt, or even have preferences. Finally, you create purely by extension of your thought without doubt or conflict. This law ensures that one way or another, you will get to that point.

**Law of cause and effect (karma).** This is easy to see its use. It simply shows you that you are an active part of All That Is, that your will has effect. As you grow, you begin to see the link between your thoughts, words, and actions with your reality. This leads to responsibility and increased power and care. This law ensures that through this process, you come to eventually know yourself as a sovereign creator. It is a gentle law that lets you build your own evidence, for whatever you believe, you will see as truth until the day you step aside and notice this link. At this point you become a Deliberate Creator.

**Law of love.** Love is the building block of all things. Love is energy. Love is not just some mushy feeling. It is energy, the actual building material of all things. It is an actual substance; in fact it is the only substance that exists, taking on the appearance of many forms. Love is also acceptance. It is acknowledging that All Things Are One. That is acceptance. The law of love ensures that you see this truth. You cannot leave an experience permanently unless you exit with love and acceptance. That is why people tend to keep repeating the same types of experiences until the day they stop hating and fighting it and instead embrace it with love and see what the situation holds for them, and heal it with love. This could be a money, health, or relationship issue. It doesn't matter. You cannot leave a situation permanently until you exit it with love. You can' t permanently get rid of what you hate; you can only leave it or transform it through love. This law ensures that you recognize the truth of unity and drop the illusions of separation.

Do you now clearly see how these laws work and how your life can be so much more effortless and prosperous simply by flowing with the laws? Why resist what you can't break? Just flow with it! Resistance creates time; acceptance creates miracles. Look at all this again, and you will see how time and effort are the creations of resistance against these unbreakable laws. For certain, flow with the laws and they will carry you where you wish to go effortlessly. They have to—they can never fail! You were not meant to struggle—struggle is unnatural.

\*     \*     \*

*You need to claim the events of your life to make yourself yours.*

**—Anne Wilson Schaef**

*Like an ability or a muscle, hearing your inner wisdom is strengthened by doing it.*

**—Robbie Gass**

*What you are, so is your world. Everything in the universe is resolved into your own inward experience. It matters little what is without, for it is all a reflection of your own state of consciousness. It matters everything what you are within, for everything without will be mirrored and colored accordingly.*

**—James Allen**

*The psychological rule says that when an inner situation is not made conscious, it happens outside, as fate. That is to say, when an individual remains undivided and does not become conscious of his inner contradictions, the world must perforce act out the conflict and be torn into opposite halves.*

**—Carl Jung**

*When the soul wishes to experience something she throws an image of the experience before her and enters into her own image.*

**—Meister Eckhart**

*Look and you will find it. What is unsought will go undetected.*

**—Anon.**

*Expect your every need to be met, expect the answer to every problem, expect abundance on every level, expect to grow spiritually.*

**—Eileen Caddy**

*Often people attempt to live their lives backwards: they try to have more things, or more money, in order to do more of what they want so that they will be happier. The way it actually works is the reverse. You must first be who you really are, then, do what you need to do, in order to have what you want.*

**—Margaret Young**

*Man can learn nothing except by going from the known to the unknown.*

**—Claude Bernard**

*A particular train of thought persisted in, be it good or bad, cannot fail to produce its results on the character and circumstances. A man cannot directly choose his circumstances, but he can choose his thoughts, and so indirectly, yet surely, shape his circumstances.*

**—James Allen**

*I bargained with life for a penny, and life would pay no more, however I begged at evening when I counted my scanty store. For life is a just employer, he gives you what you ask. But once you have set the wages, why, you must bear the task. I worked for a menial's hire, only to learn, dismayed, that any wage I had asked of Life, Life would have willingly given it.*

**—Anon.**

*To your subconscious mind the solutions to your problems of poverty is to become rich, but it is logically invalid for it to pursue this course of action if it has been told that it will make you a bad person.*

**—Simon Hall**

*To be ambitious for wealth and yet expecting to be poor; to be always doubting your ability to get what you long for, is like trying to reach east by traveling west. There is no philosophy which will help man to succeed when he is always doubting his ability to do so, and thus attracting failure.*

**—Charles Bandouin**

# You as a Feeling (Emotion)?

We have seen how your beliefs, through your feelings and emotions, create (attract by harmony) your reality, your life experiences. We have also seen how you are a band of energy, vibrating always, as all of life is.

If you were to look at yourself through eyes that see energy, you would see yourself as an energetic vibration frequency, a unique vibration that is always changing. And this is not a fairy tale; have you noticed that whenever you walk by a cheap radio, you cause interference in the reception? That is because your electromagnetic field is interfering with the radio. You are a frequency, a vibration. It is a reality.

This vibration is ever changing. What is it? The vibration is simply your feelings and emotions. That is all it is. Emotion, e-motion, is energy in motion, vibrating. That is what an emotion or feeling is or looks like. And your entire body is feeling; each of your cells feels each atom in your body feels. You are a feeling. That is your reality, and that is why it is so important to allow yourself to feel. When you block your feelings, you are literally trying to kill a part of you, and you are losing touch with reality.

Here is something interesting: Many people are afraid to feel. It terrifies them. So they avoid it, and the feeling then "converts" into "negative" thoughts and "negative" life experiences (it must find a way to express itself). Now, pain is not a feeling! *Pain is the resistance to feeling!* Isn't that an interesting paradox? That those who are afraid of feeling because they fear it hurts to feel actually end up causing pain because pain is only the resistance to feeling. When you allow yourself to feel all your feelings and emotions, the pain disappears.

The fear of feeling is the same fear of death, of ending, of catastrophe. But it is a false fear. You will not suffer or die if you allow yourself to feel. All feelings, all emotions, are neutral energy. None is good or bad. They just are. When you are afraid of a particular feeling, for whatever reasons, you judge it as "bad" and try to avoid it. This is the path to illness and death. The path to life and joy is just the other way. Allow the feeling to run its natural course unhindered and without judgment. There is nothing to do, just allow. And automatically, without you doing anything, it transmutes itself into love and joy and freedom. It might take a few seconds or minutes or hours or days or months, but it always happens that way. Simply allow without judgment, take your head off (stop thinking and intellectualizing it, living in your head), and just allow yourself to feel without judging the feeling. And this is something else you should know: When you block feelings, you literally deny them the natural travel through your body. When you allow them (like when you are lost in hearty laughter), you let them travel their natural course through the body. Their course through the body is from the solar plexus to the heart, crown, and the rest of your body, delivering energy, life force, balance, purification, and ecstasy. You can see how much you literally miss when you block and how much you gain when you allow. You can now also see how dis-ease is actually a late manifestation of denied emotional "problems."

# YOUR FREEDOM IS AT YOUR FINGERTIPS

Your freedom is yours to give away or keep for yourself; no one can "give you freedom." When you find yourself without freedom, it is not because someone has taken it away (which they cannot possibly do); it is because you have given it away. And they cannot possibly give you your freedom; only you can take it. It is yours, built in divinely. There is nothing wrong with taking and using it. It is natural and organic to do so, to express yourself uniquely as the unique expression of divinity, All That Is. And All Of It is divine.

All you have to do is OK yourself as you are. Nothing to fix; but always-eternal room to grow, to extend, to change. Recognizing that you are always and forever perfect, that there is nowhere you are going to get to, and then you become perfect and all else stops. You will, in eternity, extend, change form, and so on. But forever perfect. You are a process, not an object.

So be yourself right now and make it all OK. All of it! Feel how good and liberating that feels? Any opposition you find is simply parts of your beliefs, parts of the story you have taken on, that say it is not OK. Allow them, feel them without judgment, and stand on. They will soon transmute and free you from that judgment.

Then follow your heart. Your heart knows you the most, far better than your mind. Follow your heart. Be yourself. That is all.

\*    \*    \*

*For the rational man to hold steadfastly to his self-image ensures his abysmal ignorance. He ignores the fact that shamanism is not*

*incantations and hocus-pocus, but the freedom to perceive not only
the world taken for granted, but everything else that is humanly
possible to accomplish. He trembles at the possibility of freedom.
And freedom is at his fingertips.*

**—Carlos Castenada**

*Every living thing has been granted the power, if it so desires, to
seek an opening to freedom and go through it.*

**—Carlos Castenada**

## Quoted from the article "No Escape" by P'taah through Jani King:[2]

Beloved ones! We ask you to think of this. Is your quest for enlightenment that which is the joy and excitement of unfolding into the more of who you really are, or is it a quest to escape the fear, pain and anguish of day-to-day living in your realm? We suggest you contemplate this.

You see, my dear ones, there is no escape. **For as long as you are attempting to get rid of, overcome, release, push away, or let go of the fear, pain and anguish, that energy which you expend in pushing away will simply draw to you that which you are attempting to get away from.** What you resist will absolutely persist and what you invalidate you will absolutely empower.

What you are, indeed, is a grand embodiment of electromagnetic energy. That is, every facet of you, your physical body, your consciousness, your thoughts and beliefs and your emotional beingness are all entwined to create a body of energy which is likened unto a magnet. This energy has a resonance, a vibrational frequency, which draws to itself that which matches its own frequency.

Thusly, as you go about your day-to-day life, you create in your perceived reality those situations which reflect to you your own beliefs about who you are and how the universe is. The frequencies or resonances match. So, if you desire to bring about change in your day-to-day life, the simple fact is that you must change the frequency that you are.

We have said to you many times that **enlightenment**, or the ability to exist in that state termed fourth or fifth density as you call it, *is the natural result of loving every facet of you unconditionally*. In other words, by that unconditional love

---

[2]   See http://www.ptaah.com. Article copyright *Jani King* 2001.

you change the frequency. This is not required to be a struggle. It is simple a choice in every now. There are no magic pills or potions, no magic words, incantations or rituals. There is only love or fear. Which do you choose in any now?

Of course your frequency changes and fluctuates moment by moment. When you are in a very loving and allowing space, you perceive your outward reality from that framework. Those of you who have experienced your epiphanies or great ah-ha's have wondered why the experience has not been repeated more often, or indeed why, since you have experienced it once, can you not be in that place all of the time. Well, my dearest ones, it is because that frequency does not match who you are most of the time.

The two powerful components, if you like, of your magnetic beingness are your beliefs about yourself and the emotions attached to and underlying those beliefs. Emotions are the seat of your creative power. Where you are operating in your day to days from the fear-based emotions based on the belief that you are not worthy, not enough, powerless, love equals pain, and the universe you inhabit is a dangerous and doomed place, (any or all of the above) then your day-to-day creations will reflect this.

However, because you are powerful, wondrous beings, you change your resonance to create whatever you desire. It all starts and ends with you. Remind yourself of your grandest truth. You are in every moment, no matter the apparency, a perfect, eternal expression of Creation. You are gods and goddesses playing a wondrous game called "human life, now". The facet of you which forgets that truth, the facet which believes and feels all of that fear-based stuff, is just a little person, a tiny child who lives inside of you. One who, in spite of forgetting the grand truth, loves the totality of you absolutely; one who has struggled every day of your life to ensure that you survived; one who has always done the best possible in every circumstance. It is this little facet of you that is requiring the fullest attention, requiring your compassion and unconditional love.

We would remind you of the **keys to transformation**:

1. You can only transform what you own [what you accept; take responsibility of, responsibility = response-ability]. If there is any facet of you that you do not own, any situation that you do not own your share of, then how can you transform it?

2. You can only transform in the now. You cannot transform in your past and you cannot transform in your future. You can only transform in your now moment and the paradox of course is that when you choose transformation in your now moment, you automatically transform your past and your future.

3. You can only transform whilst you are in the emotion of the fear or pain, because that is where your power lies. If you would doubt this, then I would draw your attention to the fact that whilst you usually make your day-to-day decisions based on logic and experience, when you are in the grip of very strong emotion, your logic usually flies out the window!

4. You can only create transformation by total embracement. That is, embrace the child within who has created the undesired reality you are experiencing. Embrace the situation and the co-creators and look for the gift within this situation. If you have trouble finding the gift, remind yourself that no matter what the situation is, it is an opportunity to be the more of who you really are!

**We ask you to contemplate the fact that** *all of your fears are based on perceived lack.* **The grand truth is that there is no lack. However, as this is your belief and your fear, this is what you create in your life,** whether it is lack of love or money or creature comforts or simply ease and flow in your life. Many of you rush about in your outside world with great effort and struggle to try to change this situation and wonder why nothing changes at all, really.

The fear of lack is a resonance. The knowing of absolute abundance in every facet of your life is also a resonance. To change the resonance we suggest you would give forth joyful thanks to the universe at least once each day for the abundance in your life. Sit down and write out all the things in your life, in every area, to be thankful for. Each day as you would sing forth your thanks, feel the joy of this abundance and richness in your life. Whilst you are engaged in this activity you are in the Isness, the now, of no lack. As you go about your day you will carry this resonance with you. During your day, when you see something which pleases you or brings you joy, give forth the thanks. Stand back and be ready for change!

So you see, my dears, there is no escape. There is only you, and by your own awesome power you may create that which you desire—heaven on earth and you, the gods and goddesses, realized in the full potential called human.

I love you absolutely in your god and goddess games! Namaste.

# From Kahlil Gibran's *The Prophet*: on Freedom

And an orator said, Speak to us of Freedom.

And he answered:

At the city gate and by your fireside I have seen you prostrate yourself and worship your own freedom,

Even as slaves humble themselves before a tyrant and praise him though he slays them.

Aye, in the grove of the temple and in the shadow of the citadel I have seen the freest among you wear their freedom as a yoke and a handcuff.

And my heart bled within me; for you can only be free when even the desire of seeking freedom becomes a harness to you, and when you cease to speak of freedom as a goal and a fulfillment.

You shall be free indeed when your days are not without a care nor your nights without a want and a grief,

But rather when these things girdle your life and yet you rise above them naked and unbound.

And how shall you rise beyond your days and nights unless you break the chains which you at the dawn of your understanding have fastened around your noon hour?

In truth that which you call freedom is the strongest of these chains, though its links glitter in the sun and dazzle your eyes.

And what is it but fragments of your own self you would discard that you may become free?

If it is an unjust law you would abolish, that law was written with your own hand upon your own forehead.

112

You cannot erase it by burning your law books nor by washing the foreheads of your judges, though you pour the sea upon them.

And if it is a despot you would dethrone, see first that his throne erected within you is destroyed.

For how can a tyrant rule the free and the proud, but for a tyranny in their own freedom and a shame in their own pride?

And if it is a care you would cast off, that care has been chosen by you rather than imposed upon you.

And if it is a fear you would dispel, the seat of that fear is in your heart and not in the hand of the feared.

Verily all things move within your being in constant half embrace, the desired and the dreaded, the repugnant and the cherished, the pursued and that which you would escape.

These things move within you as lights and shadows in pairs that cling.

And when the shadow fades and is no more, the light that lingers becomes a shadow to another light.

And thus your freedom when it loses its fetters becomes itself the fetter of a greater freedom.

## From Kahlil Gibran's *The Prophet*: on Self-Knowledge

And a man said, Speak to us of Self-Knowledge.

And he answered, saying:

Your hearts know in silence the secrets of the days and the nights.

But your ears thirst for the sound of your heart's knowledge.

You would know in words that which you have always known in thought.

You would touch with your fingers the naked body of your dreams.

And it is well you should.

The hidden well-spring of your soul must needs rise and run murmuring to the sea;

And the treasure of your infinite depths would be revealed to your eyes.

But let there be no scales to weigh your unknown treasure;

And seek not the depths of your knowledge with staff or sounding line.

For self is a sea boundless and measureless.

Say not, "I have found the truth," but rather, "I have found a truth."

Say not, "I have found the path of the soul." Say rather, "I
have met the soul walking upon my path."

For the soul walks upon all paths.

The soul walks not upon a line, neither does it grow like a reed.

The soul unfolds itself, like a lotus of countless petals.

## From Kahlil Gibran's *The Prophet*: on Laws

Then a lawyer said, But what of our Laws, master?

And he answered:

You delight in laying down laws,

Yet you delight more in breaking them.

Like children playing by the ocean who build sand-towers with constancy and then destroy them with laughter.

But while you build your sand-towers the ocean brings more sand to the shore,

And when you destroy them the ocean laughs with you.

Verily the ocean laughs always with the innocent.

But what of those to whom life is not an ocean, and man-made laws are not sand-towers,

But to whom life is a rock, and the law a chisel with which they would carve it in their own likeness?

What of the cripple who hates dancers?

What of the ox who loves his yoke and deems the elk and deer of the forest stray and vagrant things?

What of the old serpent who cannot shed his skin, and calls all others naked and shameless?

And of him who comes early to the wedding feast, and when over-fed and tired goes his way saying that all feasts are violation and all feasters law-breakers?

What shall I say of these save that they too stand in the sunlight, but with their backs to the sun?

They see only their shadows, and their shadows are their laws.

And what is the sun to them but a caster of shadows?

And what is it to acknowledge the laws but to stoop down and trace their shadows upon the earth?

But you who walk facing the sun, what images drawn on the earth can hold you?

You who travel with the wind, what weather vane shall direct your course?

What man's law shall bind you if you break your yoke but upon no man's prison door?

What laws shall you fear if you dance but stumble against no man's iron chains?

And who is he that shall bring you to judgment if you tear off your garment yet leave it in no man's path?

People of Orphalese, you can muffle the drum, and you can loosen the strings of the lyre, but who shall command the skylark not to sing?

## From Kahlil Gibran's *The Prophet*: on Reason and Passion

And the priestess spoke again and said: Speak to us of Reason and Passion.

And he answered, saying:

Your soul is oftentimes a battlefield, upon which your reason and your judgment wage war against your passion and your appetite.

Would that I could be the peacemaker in your soul, that I might turn the discord and the rivalry of your elements into oneness and melody.

But how shall I, unless you yourselves be also the peacemakers, nay, the lovers of all your elements?

Your reason and your passion are the rudder and the sails of your seafaring soul.

If either your sails or your rudder be broken, you can but toss and drift, or else be held at a standstill in mid-seas.

For reason, ruling alone, is a force confining; and passion, unattended, is a flame that burns to its own destruction.

Therefore let your soul exalt your reason to the height of passion, that it may sing;

And let it direct your passion with reason, that your passion may live through its own daily resurrection, and like the phoenix rise above its own ashes.

I would have you consider your judgment and your appetite even as you would two loved guests in your house.

Surely you would not honor one guest above the other; for he who is more mindful of one loses the love and the faith of both.

Among the hills, when you sit in the cool shade of the white poplars, sharing the peace and serenity of distant fields and meadows—then let your heart say in silence, "God rests in reason."

And when the storm comes, and the mighty wind shakes the forest, and thunder and lightning proclaim the majesty of the sky,—then let your heart say in awe, "God moves in passion."

And since you are a breath in God's sphere, and a leaf in God's forest, you too should rest in reason and move in passion.

# It Is OK to Be Human. Really. That Is the Whole Point of It.

Whenever you reject any aspect of your physical human experience, you also reject an aspect of your spirit and mind. Whenever you reject any aspect of your spirit, you also reject an aspect of your physical human experience and mind. Whenever you reject any aspect of your mind, you also reject an aspect of your spirit and physical human experience. Body, mind, and spirit are one, a trinity in unity.

Think of your body as your soul in chemical clothing. Or as the denser part of your mind.

The human condition is the reason why we are here. Being human is the point of the game, so to speak. We, as spirit, did not end up on earth to suffer, or as a punishment. The long-term divine goal, so to speak, is to evolve humanity to a level where we are fully conscious, even physically, of Who We Really Are and are able to experience the bliss, power, love, and abundance of Spirit, Who We Really Are. In a sense, we as the human race are somewhere in the adolescent stage of evolution, almost moving into the adult stage and finally the maturity stage.

You cannot view the human experience as unworthy and hope to have self-fulfillment because that view is already against your life purpose. The human condition, with its amazing range of aspects, is one that is to be fully embraced and loved as this is the only way to move it forward. You cannot reject yourself, your body, or your life and then look outside of it for salvation and hope to get it. Whenever you reject any aspect of your physical human experience, you also automatically reject an aspect of your spirit and mind. Accepting does not mean agreeing with or even liking. It is simply accepting, allowing, not resisting. If you don't like something you are experiencing, choose differently. Choosing differently does not require rejecting what you don't choose.

Part of the cultural story we live in says that there is something wrong with humans, or aspects of humanity are against God, or whatever. It is similar to saying that an ant cannot be a good ant unless it strives not to be an ant. Amazingly, you cannot know your Creator if you do not know yourself, and you cannot know yourself if you deny yourself. So strangely it may seem, the very ideas that humans use to reach God actually separate them from God—and the results in the physical world demonstrate this as well. The shame of being human is extremely toxic. It says there is something wrong with you as a human *because you are human.* It is just an idea, yet it is believed in by much of the human race, with disastrous consequences. Let the ant be the ant, the fly be the fly, the fish be the fish, and the human be the human. There is no mistake in their perfect construction; and their purpose is to experience who they are, as they are, all aspects of divinity, creations of divinity, divinity itself manifesting in a variety of forms for the sake of self-experience. It is all divine! That is an alternative perspective to the painful and judgmental one that says that it is all wrong and in need of "fixing."

# Part 3

## The Practice Revisited

# THE PRACTICE ONCE AGAIN

## All of Life Is Cyclic

All of life is cyclic. The in and out of breath, day and night, on and off, up and down, money goes in and out, up and down—most people try to "stay" in one part of this natural cycle and "avoid" the other part. No one can do that, yet millions attempt it. Life being black and white, they play a game called white must win! (or black must win!), and this just doesn't work no matter how hard you try. What you can do, however, is to understand the cycles and flow, flow, with them. With understanding, you can stand suffering free from the cycles and live a fruitful life.

Money can teach us a lot about the cycles of life. Let us look at the stock market for a moment:

Here is a chart of the U.S. markets since the 1930s (actually, it is a chart of all the companies in the stock market that make up the Dow Jones Industrial Average). What do you notice? (By the way, you can do these charts yourself free on *Yahoo! Finance*, which is where these charts were taken from.) Look at this chart:

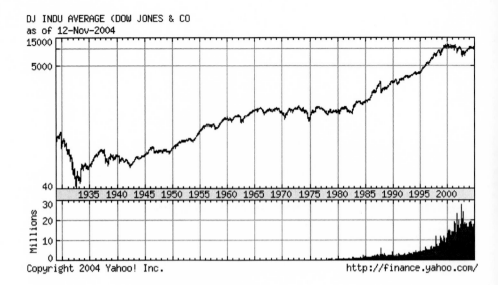

DJ INDU AVERAGE (DOW JONES & CO
as of 12-Nov-2004

http://finance.yahoo.com/

It trends up generally from the 1930s till today, but it doesn't do that in a straight line, does it? It waves up and down, up and down. By the laws of nature, the laws of mathematics, it must wave up and down. Why? Well, for many reasons. For example, let us assume there is a company in there that is worth $1 million (this is an example only, so let us use a low figure we can work with). This company has one million shares distributed, so each share is intrinsically worth $1 because if you were to break up the company and sell its assets, you would get $1 million; and you would have to divide that million dollars by a million shares and give each shareholder $1 per share. Now, in the stock market, there will be people buying the shares in anticipation that the company will grow in value in the future, so they are willing to pay a bit more than $1 per share. And so the price would rise, but if it gets up too high (say to $2 a share), these optimistic buyers would now start to think that it is too expensive to profit from. So they would stop buying. Now the people offering the share for $2 would, sooner or later, need cash to feed themselves and their families, and so they would start lowering their price and sell the stock for less than $2; and the price would keep dropping until it reached a point where the buyers would again see it as a bargain (say, at $0.80 a share) and start buying it up again, driving the price up again. This is just one simple example of how nature and mathematics combine to keep prices swinging up and down within very definite boundaries. It works not just in the stock market but also in all areas that concern money. Even in your personal life, you earn money but find that you must spend it to eat, get shelter, and so on (nature compels you). Yet you cannot spend more than you earn and hold in debt, and you cannot earn more than what you are generating with your financial wisdom and application (mathematics compels you). You can alter how you position yourself in regard to the cycles (thereby finding degrees of freedom and profit/loss), but you cannot stop the cycles.

Now, let us look at a different chart. Go back to the chart on top and notice how the last five years there look like. We will now magnify that five-year segment of the same above chart. Here is a chart of the last five years (the last five years of the chart we just saw above). What do you notice? Look.

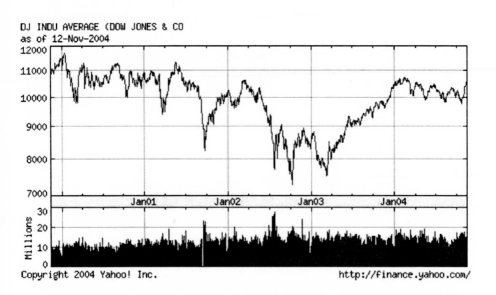

The same waves! Up and down they go!

Now magnify the last one year of these five years and see what happens:

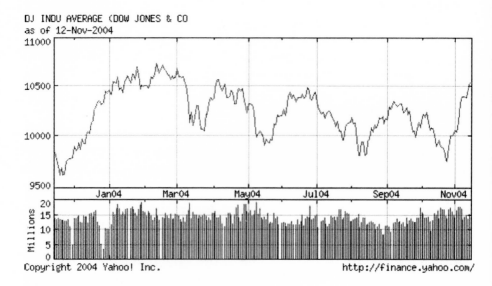

The same waves! Up and down they go!

Now, magnify the last six months of this year and see what happens:

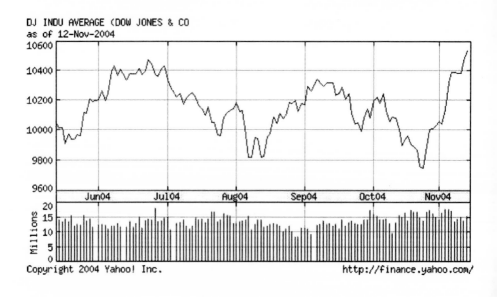

The same waves! Up and down they go!

Now, magnify the last three months of this last six months and see what happens:

The same waves! Up and down they go!

Now notice how straight the last few days on the chart above look like. The chart seems to have a straight line moving up. Now magnify the last five days of this and see what happens:

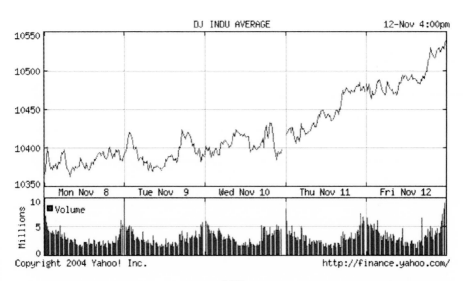

The same waves! Up and down they go!

Now look at the last day in the chart above and notice that it has movement but not as frantic as when you magnify the last one day of this as follows:

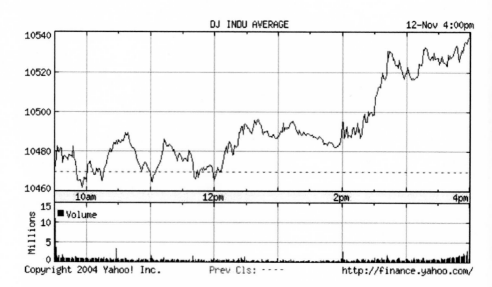

If you were to magnify this one-day chart above and focus on just one hour, you would see that the activity is also quite busy. The cycles of money never cease. They are one within the other, one within the other. They are fractal in nature.

Now that you can see that money moves in waves of up and down, like the ocean currents, you can finally stop taking it personally when you experience the downside of these natural cycles. It isn't you who is failing when you hit a downtime; it is simply that you are experiencing a natural phenomenon. However, you can arrange yourself so that you experience it differently (i.e., with less pain or even with profit).

This is worth repeating: *the dualities of life must always exist together.* Hot and cold exist together. Tall and short exist together. Night and day exist together. So does having and not having. The experience called having is impossible without the *existence* of the experience called not having. In the absence of that which is not, that which is, is not. That is why we live in a relative world. So you will do a very good service to your mind and emotions if you accepted that you couldn't change this aspect of creation no matter how much you tried. And it isn't "your fault" that creation works like this (in other words, don't take it personally, you didn't fail). However, (1) *you do not have to personally experience not having so that you can experience having* (all that is required is that the experience exists somewhere in the universe) and (2) you can set yourself up so that you experience much more of having and "insulate" yourself from not having (e.g., through savings and investment systems) and even profit from the "not having" part of an economic cycle (e.g., making money when the market is falling).

To put it all in another way,

1. Life is a Whole that is composed of both the negative and positive sides of that whole.

2. Both sides are integral and necessary to the whole.

3. Life swings from one polarity to the next but in different phases. Take money for example. There is an inflow and an outflow. That is natural to the flow. Both have benefits. Income allows you to be rewarded for the value you put out, and outflow allows you to reward others and at the same time get things you did not have. However, the lack of understanding of any one side brings imbalance. And resisting any one side brings imbalance. What are other expressions of outflow? Debt? Yes, that is one. So is debt bad? No. Debt allows you to make space for more abundance later. And are bills bad? No. They allow your service provider to give you services you choose and then get payment for them later. However, misunderstanding yourself in relation to debt can cause big trouble for you. For example, if you label yourself as bad and incapable just because of debts or bills you have, you have not understood the true nature of cause and effect in this system, and you have diminished yourself. So your experience with debt and bills would be fearful. But once you understand it all, then you remain the same wise and calm and joyful person regardless of which part of the cycle you are in, and you also no

longer get into trouble with debts and bills. With understanding, you become able to enjoy prosperity at all times and comfortably and happily live with debt coming in and out of life. Just to make this clear, the very wealthy people in this world also have debts, but the difference between them and the poor guy with debts is that they are solid and integral with themselves regardless, and so debt actually helps them! See, debt gives you the capacity to make space for greater abundance later; but the flip side, if you don't understand yourself and the laws of cause and effect, is that it can swallow you.

4. And thus the way out is, once again, in embracing all aspects of life and then understanding your True Self in relation to them, and finally understanding the true nature of cause and effect.

5. That cycle of life, from one side to the other, has to keep going. You cannot stop it, so why bother resist? Why bother? The only thing you can do is experience it differently. Instead of experiencing the doom of the negative side, experience the boom of it. Every negative side has massive benefits. Negative does not mean bad. For example, instead of experiencing the debt kind of outflow of money with pain, you can experience it with pleasure; for it can teach you much about making wealth, about who your Really Are, and give you capital with which to have even more money than you ever had!

Here is a symbol that represents all this very well, a symbol that you have no doubt seen before:

The yin and yang, positive and negative, male and female, up and down, on and off—all making up the whole, flowing into each other.

Enough about money. The point is that life is dualistic, cyclic.

Good and bad is a perspective, a point of view. It is a value judgment made personally depending on where you stand and what you wish to achieve. "Bad" and "good" things happen to everyone. This has absolutely nothing to do with whether you are a good person or a bad person. Remember, good and bad is a value judgment based on a point of view, a perspective. It also has nothing to do with how much care you have taken into planning your life and controlling it. You see, you do create your reality, you do achieve the goals you set and align with. But the path to those points is always twisting and turning, all of it wonderfully designed to take you to your destination. The path is winding through the polarities of life, and at any one point, you may call part of the path "good" and part of it "bad"; and later you may look back and say, "Actually, that bad turned out to be good, and vice versa," proving yet again, that good and bad are value judgments depending on where you stand. The point being, life gives you what you desire and align with, but the path that takes you there is wonderfully created to purposely weave through the polarities of life. So relax.

> *All human life has its seasons and cycles, and no one's personal chaos can be permanent. Winter, after all, gives way to spring and summer though sometimes when branches stay dark and the earth cracks with ice, one thinks they will never come, that spring, and that summer, but they do, and always.*

> **—Truman Capote**

> *The world is not to be put in order; the world is order, incarnate. It is for us to harmonize with this order.*

> **—Henry Miller**

Let us explore duality (polarity) in life in a little more detail:

I would like you to notice something else about nature. It all has a foundation on seven energy bases. Look at colors. There are seven primary colors (the seven colors of the rainbow). All other colors are made up by mixing these seven primary colors. Look at sounds.

There are seven sounds (do, re, mi, fa, so, la, ti). All other sounds are made up by mixing these seven sounds and going up or down in pitch and so on, which simply means having the same sound at a higher frequency/wavelength multiple.

An interesting property of energy is to do with **vibration frequency**. The higher you go in vibration frequency of these colors and sounds, the higher, stronger, yet less perceptible they become. The lower you go with the frequency, the weaker, heavier, and more perceptible they become until they fall off our sensory range. An example of high-frequency, powerful sounds and light is ultrasound and X-rays.

Another interesting property is **duality**. Each of these seven has dual states (on/off, positive/negative, good/bad, light/dark, male/female, and whatever else you wish to call it). This duality is what allows that very thing to be known. You know the positive because the negative exists, and the positive can only be created and experienced within the field of the negative. Form and no form. You cannot experience tall without having a concept of short. And both need to exist for the thing known as height to exist. You cannot experience cold without having a concept of hot. And both need to exist for the thing known as temperature to exist. Hence, negative is not to be avoided as such, but embraced. As you will soon see, what you resist persists, what you embrace empowers you and releases you. Although this book asks that you drop negative patterns, it does *not* seek to do so by asking you to *disown and cast away* negatives. Instead, it asks you to stop living in a negative imbalance, in a predominantly negative pattern. It asks you to know yourself positively as well and embrace both. In such a state, the combination and acceptance of the duality as all part of you enable you to achieve the state of "the whole is greater than the sum of the parts," a state of transcendence. It is somewhat like a bird. If a bird has any one of its wings, it cannot fly. It doesn't matter which wing it has, if it is only one; it will not fly. But given both wings, it takes off, and the whole becomes greater than the sum of the parts.

*Embrace all polarities, disown none, and you will transcend and become wholly powerful.*

Another interesting property is **resonance**. Energy resonates and attracts with similar energy. Unlike energy repels. It even sounds appropriately harmonious or unharmonious were you to hear it (like in music)! And were you to see unlike energy coming together, for example as waves in a laboratory experiment, you would see that it has the appropriate interference or constructiveness. Like energy always attracts like energy and vice versa. You always create and attract external conditions (including health) that mirror your internal state. As you change that state, you will notice the external conditions falling away and new ones coming in that reflect your new state. Sometimes this falling away can be sudden if your change is big, and it might scare you and make you feel as if you are losing things. But relax knowing that it is natural, healthy, and normal; and it is giving way to something that is more like your new self.

Here is something that will help you tremendously in your understanding of your life and transforming it as you wish:

*In this universe, created by a perfectly powerful and capable Creator, absolutely nothing exists in chaos, disorder, and accident. And you are created in the image and likeness of this Creator (remember, you are spirit with a body that responds exactly to mind instructions).*

*Being in the image and likeness of this Creator, you are infinitely powerful, abundant, peaceful, and perfect in the exact same way. You may have forgotten this, but evolution and growth are all about remembering what you already are. Step-by-step, you realize higher aspects of yourself. You remember. As such, there is nothing new to learn. All you are doing is unlearning the original error, step-by-step, at whatever rate you choose.*

*Everything works perfectly with precision according to universal laws. It is impossible to create chaos as that would mean undoing the eternal design put forth by an infinitely intelligent life force.*

*However, it is very possible and commonplace to judge things as chaotic. When you judge a thing as chaotic (something that "should not have happened"), you throw your very own self into chaos.*

*Your judgment of life's situations as chaotic things happening to you is what strips you of your power to see the reason behind the situation and to respond effectively and positively to it.*

*At this judgment point, you create stress in your life. You also split your personality into two, one which you wish to hide and run away from, and another that you feel has been victimized. This is the root cause of all disease, suffering, and pain; and it is totally unnecessary and preventable.*

*Your illusionary perception can be corrected by your decision to acknowledge that everything is in order. Once you acknowledge that, you can now look behind the event to see the reason.*

*Within that reason is a seed to your highest growth, healing, and accomplishment! Indeed, healing is merely the revealing and acknowledgement of the perfect truth underneath all the illusion.*

*Let us create Man in our own image and likeness.*

**—Genesis**

Here is another way of looking at it. Imagine that this is the graph of your life:

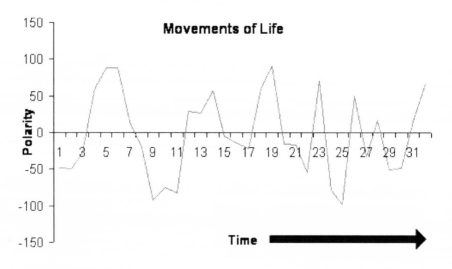

As you can see above, as time moves on, your life flows up and down between the "positive" and "negative" polarities (please, please keep in mind that positive does not necessarily mean good, nor does negative necessarily mean bad; it is just polarity, opposites).

Now we all have goals, don't we? We all have desires. And our desires, when we align with them, always get fulfilled. Now here is the same chart showing the points at which various goals are fulfilled:

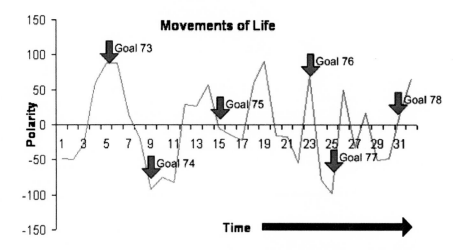

The point is that you get your desires manifested, but the path that takes you to them is winding, winding through the polarities of life.

Consider this:

*It's all in how you look at things.*

*There is no such thing as bad weather, only different kinds of good weather.*

*The problem is not that there are problems. The problem is thinking that having problems is a problem.*

*Hard times are inevitable, but misery is optional.*

## Practice, Practice, Practice. Play, Play, Play.

At the beginning, all this may be hard for you to do if you have been used to living differently, to resisting. But as with any other skill, you get better with practice; at the beginning, you don't know how to do it, let alone do it well. But with each new time you practice, each time you do it once more, you get better and better. Eventually, you become a natural, a master! So don't look for shortcuts, and don't be impatient; just be gentle with yourself and keep at it. You will naturally get better and better. No rush.

And **most importantly**, PLAY! Play with this. Don't take it seriously; don't be hard with yourself. Take it as play and have some humor. Laugh at yourself rather than beat yourself up. Play, play, play. Play is always the best way to learn. There are no mistakes, only learning opportunities. And you don't have to be perfect. So play with this.

> *Man is most nearly himself when he achieves the seriousness of a child at play.*

> **—Heraclitus, Greek philosopher (535-475 BCE)**

So be who you are; it is your key to power and liberation.

I Am That I Am.

Here are a few quotes to inspire you:

> *Genuine beginnings begin within us, even when they are brought to our attention by external opportunities.*

> **—William Bridges**

> *To know what you prefer instead of humbly saying Amen to what the world tells you you ought to prefer, is to have kept your soul alive.*

> **—Robert Louis Stevenson**

*We will discover the nature of our particular genius when we stop
trying to conform to our own or to other people's models, learn to
be ourselves, and allow our natural channel to open.*

**—Shakti Gawain**

*All you need to do to receive guidance is to ask for it and then
listen.*

**—Sanaya Roman**

*It is not because things are difficult that we do not dare; it is because
we do not dare that they are difficult.*

**—Seneca**

*Man can learn nothing except by going from the known to the
unknown.*

**—Claude Bernard**

*Often people attempt to live their lives backwards: they try to have
more things, or more money, in order to do more of what they want
so that they will be happier. The way it actually works is the reverse.
You must first be who you really are, then, do what you need to do,
in order to have what you want.*

**—Margaret Young**

*He who knows others is wise; he who knows himself is
enlightened.*

**—Lao Tzu**

*To keep the body in good health is a duty . . . Otherwise we shall
not be able to keep our mind strong and clear.*

**—Buddha**

*You cannot fear your own being and expect to travel through it, to explore its dimensions.*

**—Seth**

*The good news is that, the moment you decide that what you know is more important than what you have been taught to believe, you will have shifted gears in your quest for abundance. Success comes from within, not from without. It begins by listening to your inner calling and wisdom.*

**—Ralph Waldo Emerson**

*To your subconscious mind the solutions to your problems of poverty is to become rich, but it is logically invalid for it to pursue this course of action if it has been told that it will make you a bad person.*

**—Simon Hall**

*Empty your mind. Be formless, shapeless. Like water. You put water in a cup, it becomes the cup. You put water in a bottle, it becomes the bottle. You put it in a teapot, it becomes the teapot. Now, water can flow, or it can crash. Be water, my friend.*

**—Bruce Lee**

*The root of a bulb which shall produce a white lily is an unsightly thing; one might look upon it with disgust. But how foolish we should be to condemn the bulb for its appearance when we know the lily is within it. The root is perfect after its kind; it is a perfect but incomplete lily, and so we must learn to look upon every man and woman, no matter how unlovely in outward manifestation; they are perfect in their stage of being and they are becoming complete. Behold, it is all very good . . . It will make an immense difference with your faith and spirit whether you look upon civilization as a good thing which is becoming better or as a bad and evil thing which is decaying. One viewpoint gives you an advancing and expanding mind and the other gives you a descending and decreasing mind. One viewpoint will make you grow greater and the other will inevitably cause you to grow smaller. One will enable you to work for the eternal things; to do large works in a great way toward the completing of all that is incomplete and inharmonious; and the other will make you a mere patchwork reformer, working almost without hope to save a few lost souls from what you will grow to consider a lost and doomed world. So you see it makes a vast difference to you, this matter of the social viewpoint. "All's right with the world. Nothing can possibly be wrong but my personal attitude, and I will make that right. I will see the facts of nature and all the events, circumstances, and conditions of society, politics, government, and industry from the highest viewpoint. It is all perfect, though incomplete. It is all the handiwork of God; behold, it is all very good."*

**—James Allen**

*Whoever undertakes to set himself up as a judge of Truth and Knowledge is shipwrecked by the laughter of the gods.*

**—Albert Einstein**

*Problems are only opportunities in work clothes.*

**—Henry J. Kaiser**

*If you don't like something, change it. If you can't change it, change your attitude. Hard times are inevitable, but misery is optional.*

# WE NEED YOUR TESTIMONIALS AND STORIES!

Yes! You really do us and the world a great service when you share your experiences! So please do share them! It will only take you a few minutes. Simply tell us what your experience has been, and we will let the world know. It helps us in knowing how we are serving you, and it helps other people in gaining confidence in our materials and knowing that they can help them just as they helped you. So please, don't be shy! ☺ Go for it here:

*http://RevolutionScape.com*

### And For More . . .

Many other life-changing books and software, plus affiliate/reseller income opportunities, are available at *http://RevolutionScape.com.*

# And for Peace of Mind

For peace of mind, we need to resign as general manager of the universe. - *Larry Eisenberg*

# INDEX

# L

# M

# N

# O

# P

# R

# S

CPSIA information can be obtained at www.ICGtesting.com
Printed in the USA
LVOW072036151211

259596LV00002B/165/P